82 122217183

Dorothy Moriarty lives in Camberley in Surrey. She has contributed to the Help the Aged handbook *Take Care of Yourself* (1988), and has broadcast on *Woman's Hour* and appeared twice on *Wogan*. She visits America, where some of her family live, twice a year, and has appeared on American television.

D0237947

DOROTHY

The Memoirs of a Nurse 1889 – 1989

Dorothy Moriarty

CORGI BOOKS

DOROTHY
A CORGI BOOK 0 552 99463 4

Originally published in Great Britain by Sidgwick & Jackson Ltd

PRINTING HISTORY
Sidgwick & Jackson edition published 1989
Corgi edition published 1991

All rights reserved
Copyright © Dorothy Moriarty 1989

The right of Dorothy Moriarty to be identified as author of this
work has been asserted in accordance with sections 77 and 78
of the Copyright Designs and Patents Act 1988.

Conditions of sale
1. This book is sold subject to the condition that it shall
not, by way of trade *or otherwise*, be lent, re-sold, hired
out or otherwise circulated in any form of binding or cover
other than that in which it is published *and without a similar
condition including this condition being imposed on the
subsequent purchaser*.
2. This book is sold subject to the Standard Conditions of
Sale of Net Books and may not be re-sold in the UK below the
net price fixed by the publishers for the book.

This book is set in 10/11pt Times by
County Typesetters, Margate, Kent

Corgi Books are published by Transworld Publishers Ltd.,
61–63 Uxbridge Road, Ealing, London W5 5SA, in Australia
by Transworld Publishers (Australia) Pty. Ltd., 15-23 Helles
Avenue, Moorebank, NSW 2170, and in New Zealand by
Transworld Publishers (N.Z.) Ltd., Cnr. Moselle and
Waipareira Avenues, Henderson, Auckland.

Made and printed in Great Britain by
Cox & Wyman Ltd, Reading, Berks.

To my family.

To the memory of the colleagues who shared
these days of training.

To the wonderful friends wherever they are,
without whom there would have been no icing
on the cake.

Contents

Foreword

I first met Dorothy Moriarty when she was ninety-eight years old and I was a minister in the Department of Health. She had been helping with a booklet written for the first time for elderly people themselves, called *Take Care of Yourself*. Dorothy's contribution was a section for the *very* old. It included good advice on how to look one's best and how to travel in comfort to America at an advanced age. She was writing even then with the lively, humorous style which fills the pages which follow.

This lady, I thought to myself, is clearly something rather special. I made contact with her again and she sent me part of this manuscript. Within a few minutes reading, it was obvious her memories must not be lost. I am truly delighted to see them now in print, so that we can all share her insights, her joys and sorrows, the days as a young nurse, the awakening of love, the pleasures and miseries of life in the days when Victoria's reign was still a bright and recent memory.

Dorothy is one of the most remarkable women I have ever met. I hope you enjoy the story of these days long gone as much as I have.

Edwina Currie MP
July 1989

Part One
Childhood

1

I still have the gold brooch with '1888' outlined in seed pearls that was the bridegroom's gift to the bride when Bernard Bishop married Alice Maule in London, over a hundred years ago. I was born the following year, in Russell Road, Kensington, apparently a sickly child, for I also have the Royal Doulton salad bowl that served as a christening font at my emergency baptism. My mother poetically chose the name Dorothy, 'the gift of God', for me, but this was degraded to Dolly, or Doll, by the two brothers, Cuthbert and Carteret, who soon followed into the sheltered and comfortable world of an upper-middle-class family.

Carteret was a dream baby, with pink-and-white complexion, blue eyes, and tight red-gold curls that covered his head and hung down in ringlets. When he was four, the curls were cut off and he was promoted from a kilt-like skirt to knickerbockers. I think my mother loved those curls. Years later I found one hidden in the back of her gold locket. Cuthbert was the sturdy type, a male chauvinist in miniature. And I was a skinny child, with eyes that were grey-blue or green, depending on the light, and hair that was gold and fine and hung straight to my shoulders. An aunt once said, 'That child would be quite pretty, Alice, if she were not so sallow,' and this careless remark so spoiled my image that I saw myself as an ugly duckling forever after.

We lived in a tall house in Avonmore Road, not far from where I was born. Right at the top were three rooms; a nursery and night nursery that had bars to the windows to keep us from hanging out, and a small bedroom where Nanny slept on her treasured feather bed, an heirloom from her girlhood on a Kentish farm. When you lay on it, it would close round you, snug and warm.

Those lovely London days! They were never dull, from the early morning light with its twittering of sparrows under the

13

eaves and the cry of the 'hot rolls' boy, to the blue and misty darkness that brought the lamplighter. We would wait for him, our noses pressed against the cold glass of the window pane, and shout, 'He's coming', as a humped little man carrying a small ladder came into view. We watched as he propped his ladder against each lamppost and climbed to pull the chain of the pilot light with a hooked stick. This humble figure, light by light, created the magic of a great city.

In winter there was the muffin man, a baize-covered tray on his head, ringing his handbell and crying, 'Muffins and crumpets', as he walked along. Sometimes Rose, the house-parlourmaid, would dash up the area steps, capstrings flying, to intercept him and get muffins for our tea. Those were the days when we got out the big toasting fork and crowded round Nanny as she speared the muffins and held them close to the glowing coals of the nursery fire. Then they were buttered and transferred to the tea table, where home-made cake and jam were set ready for the meal we liked best of all.

When tea was over, we got ready for the high spot of the day. In the nursery, the boys wore plain linen overalls to protect the blouses of the sailor suits which were worn by all pre-school boys of those days, and I wore a sleeveless linen pinafore. After these were removed, and we had washed our hands and faces, we went downstairs to the drawing room.

Mother, dressed in a tea gown garnished with lace or chiffon ruffles, lay on the long sofa in the drawing room and belonged only to us for one enchanted hour. She was a person set apart and yet intimately our own. Never demonstrative, her kisses were rare and occasions to be remembered – like the nights she and Father would go out to dine or dance, and she would come up to the night nursery, a shining figure in silk or satin, with the light from the dying fire flickering on her as she bent to kiss us. A magic moment that gave peace and security. She was a dream love, who told us stories 'out of her own head' as we phrased it, and unlocked the cupboard where our best toys were kept.

Our father was a stockbroker and, I suspect, not a very good one. William Henry Bishop, our grandfather, was a successful man with two sons who had refused to go into the family business, two daughters who were nuns, an unmarried daughter who looked after him, and Bernard – our father – who was roped into the firm with no choice of another career. Careers

14

considered fit for gentlemen were restricted in those days, and so Bernard became a member of the London Stock Exchange, and the pawn of an autocratic father.

His escape was into the world of antiques, especially clocks and watches. His greatest friend was an old watchmaker in Clerkenwell, whom we children knew as 'Uncle Parsons'. I shall never forget the blissful day when I was introduced to this mythical character.

Uncle Parsons' shop was a small and dingy one in a basement. Three steps down and you were in an Aladdin's cave of shining metal pieces – the insides of disembowelled clocks and watches. Dozens of little brass wheels reflected the light from a couple of gas lamps, one of which was fixed over a bench where a bearded figure, removing a watchmaker's glass from one eye, looked up and greeted us.

'Good morning, sir, and let the little lady be seated. Tom—' Upon which, out of the shadows, appeared the apprentice. A small boy, scarcely older than myself, swiftly wiped the seat of a hard chair in deference to my smart new fur-trimmed pelisse.

The old man rose from his bench, wiped his hands on a bit of cotton waste, and solemnly shook hands, first with Father and then with me, as I hastily withdrew a hand from the fur muff hanging round my neck by a cord. It was a cold and cheerless day in mid-November: my birthday.

'And now, sir, you've come for the watch. It's ready and waiting for the young lady. Tom,' he ordered the small boy waiting uneasily in the back of the shop, 'bring me the parcel from the top shelf yonder.' On my father's nod I opened the parcel with trembling fingers – my first watch, a little silver one on a silver chain. It was a proud moment when he hung it round my neck.

My father was associated with highlights like this. He gave me my first diary, and a diary became an annual present. He took us to the circus and to the pantomime. But he was seldom part of our daily lives. He was a tall dapper man with a fair handlebar moustache. Across his waistcoat gleamed a looped gold watch chain, and when we were very small he would pull his gold half-hunter out of his pocket and make it chime the hour for our delight. As far as day-to-day life was concerned, he remained a remote figure who disappeared every morning, and returned in the evening when Nanny was filling up the big hip

15

bath, or perhaps the little saucer bath, with hot water for our nightly bathe. A hip bath was one in which you sat nose-to-chin; a saucer bath was a shallow circular one in which, having been well soaped by Nanny, you trickled yourself clean with water squeezed from a sponge. We thought the saucer bath more fun.

Our down-to-earth love was Nanny. In those early years she ruled our lives, a gentle dictator. She was a small brown woman, with the eyes of a faithful spaniel overhung by black eyebrows whose fierceness deceived no-one. The nannies of those days were a section of society set apart, dedicated, rather like nuns. They 'took service' as young girls, in a family of the middle or upper class, and became an integral part of that family. Having ruled the nursery in one generation, they nearly always transferred to the nursery of the second or even third. They seldom retired, but went into a sort of semi-retirement of sewing and darning and counselling, finally earning a modest tombstone in some green churchyard. *The loyal friend and companion of such and such a family*. Which, indeed, they were.

Our Nanny was Grace Wood, but no-one ever called her that. She was a simple country girl of seventeen when she came to look after the babies of a country parson. My mother's father was rector of Cheam in Surrey, and when he died, Nanny and his widow brought up the family. She lasted through Grandmother's conversion to Catholicism, and came to my mother when I was born. Years later, when Cuthbert was married and had children, she went to them.

Nanny had no nurserymaid under her, for my father was neither nobility nor landed gentry. My mother never rated a parlourmaid; she had to make do with a combination known as a house-parlourmaid, and Cook was a cook-general. This sounds grander than it was; it merely meant that there was no kitchen maid under her, and Cook had to prepare her own vegetables. She also took on some of the duties of a housemaid.

All in all, our status symbols were not very impressive. Nevertheless, our mother did go visiting with her card case, a dainty affair in ivory and mother-of-pearl.

'Not at home, Madam.'

The parlourmaid, having said this, would tender a silver tray, on to which mother dropped three cards from her white kid gloved hand: her own for the lady and two of my father's, which were smaller bits of pasteboard. One of his was also for the lady; the other (as one male chauvinist to another) was for her lord and master. When I grew older, Mother sometimes took me with her to pay these calls; it was part of a girl's training. But I would only sit in a corner of the drawing room, wishing I could be doing something more exciting.

When we were small, a daily walk was part of the nursery routine. Nanny often took us to Holland Park, where there were benches to sit on and other nannies with whom she could chat. The big trees of Holland Park were our inspiration and delight. Some of them had sizeable hollows in their trunks, so that we could play 'houses'. Children grew up slowly in those days, and make-believe supplied the food for imagination now taken over by radio and television.

Sometimes we played tricks on Nanny to relieve the boredom of sedate behaviour. One of these tricks was the surreptitious sailing of paper boats in the horse troughs. These granite monstrosities were monuments to our national love of animals; underneath the big trough for horses was one for thirsty dogs. For humans there was a press-button spout on the side and an iron cup on a chain. When we saw our objective looming up, Cuthbert and I lagged behind and, pausing beside the trough, launched our paper boats, lingering as long as we dared to watch their hazardous voyage. On our return journey we ran eagerly to see if they had sunk or perhaps been swallowed by a horse.

In the spring we had peg tops and whipping tops. Peg tops were pear-shaped. One wound string round them, and then, with a quick flick of the wrist, threw them on the ground, where they revolved on a metal foot. The whipping tops were squat little things that were literally whipped into spinning.

With autumn, out came our wooden hoops. We bowled them along the public footways with little wooden sticks, while Nanny and the baby in his pram followed sedately behind. When Carteret, the baby, grew into a toddler, a mailcart constructed on the lines of a dogcart replaced the pram. It had a wooden seat divided by a board so that two children could sit back to back, and two big wooden wheels. The shafts were firmly gripped by Nanny as she trudged along in her elastic-sided boots and neat grey uniform.

London streets had their special interests and excitements. A Punch and Judy show, for instance. Of course we joined the

17

crowd, mostly of small children with their nannies. The show seldom varied, yet never palled. We liked violence, like the modern child, and Punch's stick going 'whack, whack' supplied it in full measure. Once or twice we met up with a dancing bear being led along by a chain in the park. When a few spectators assembled, the poor shambling creature rose on its hind legs and slowly revolved around its master, who held the chain with one hand and played the mouth organ with the other. We all clapped with delight until dragged away by Nanny. Fortunately, dancing bears were becoming a rarity, but barrel-organ monkeys were quite common. The monkey collected pennies in its little feathered hat, while its eyes held a silent indictment of the indignity of its braided skirt and jacket. If, at the master's instigation, it shook hands with you, that meant you put sixpence into the hat with the jaunty feather. I shivered to feel the monkey's little paw gripping my hand.

Then there was the pavement artist drawing portraits of the Royal Family and scenes of country life, which owed little to nature and much to the artist's vivid imagination and lurid chalks. We dropped our pennies into the cap laid beside him and were sad to think that the first shower would wipe away his beautiful pictures. Sometimes we met a funeral and stood respectfully as the slow procession passed: carriages drawn by black horses with nodding plumes on their heads; the coffin in the glass-cased hearse, piled high with wreaths; the mutes, men wearing top hats with crêpe streamers, walking beside it. Cuthbert, sulky, would be made to take off his hat.

'You must learn to be respectful to the dead,' Nanny told him as she tweaked the elastic from under his chin.

Other times there was the awe-inspiring sight of straw laid down in the road to deaden the clip-clop of horses' hooves and the rattle of iron-rimmed wheels before a house that had someone lying sick in the front room. Perhaps dying. 'Why is noise bad for them, Nanny? Will the sick person die?' We knew the answer would be found on the front doorknocker, where a knot of black crêpe would be tied when someone inside died. But children ask questions for the sake of asking. And Nanny always had an answer. Like the time Cuthbert wanted to know if the one-legged man who sold matches and bootlaces from a tray slung round his neck would find his leg waiting for him in heaven.

'His leg is buried in a battlefield,' Nanny answered, 'but you may be sure the whole of him will stand before the Lord on Judgement Day.'

I was labelled delicate. I cannot imagine why, unless the idea stemmed from my emergency christening over the salad bowl. I was also supposed to be precocious, and therefore it was decided that my education could wait until my skinny body filled out and my sallow cheeks took on some healthy pinkness. But I was determined to learn to read, and when we went for walks I would secrete a piece of chalk to copy a word here and there from shop windows, using my black stockings as a blackboard. Then I enquired of Nanny, 'What does this say?' Nanny, whose tolerance accepted even writing on stockings, supplied the answer, with criticisms if needed.

Eventually, our mother gave us lessons. Our equipment was a slate framed in wood with a sponge attached by string to one corner, a slate pencil that squeaked delightfully if pressed hard, and copy books which we filled with pothooks and commas. At mid-morning we had a break for milk and biscuits while our mother sipped a glass of sherry. Apart from these lessons, we were free as the sparrows, hopping about and finding our own crumbs of amusement.

I have often wondered how our mother spent her days then. I know she was a great reader, and she also did embroidery, but she had no shopping to do, apart from rare visits to London to buy clothes and shoes. The butcher, the baker (his basket filled with loaves of all shapes and sizes), and the greengrocer each waited, cap in hand, to take the orders Cook had scribbled on her slate. She and Mother went into conference every morning, my mother still sitting at the breakfast table from which my father had departed for his mysterious life in the City. Sometimes they would visit the larder, inspecting leftovers laid out on the cool marble shelves, checking the neatly labelled brown crockery or glass storage jars. One enormous jar that stood on the stone floor was filled with eggs preserved in pickling fluid. Wire covers were placed over meat joints, replacing the shining metal ones under which they had been brought to the dining table. Cook's larder was a long way from the refrigerator my granddaughters raid so happily today.

Germs must have had a most wonderful and carefree existence in those days. The milk Nanny poured over our breakfast porridge came from cows that browsed happily in fields and meadows, untroubled by inspectors and tuberculin tests, and were milked by hand (not always surgically clean hands, I'm sure). From the milking pail our milk was poured into great pewter churns, and finally brought to our door by a friendly milkman driving a horse-drawn float that resembled a Roman chariot, or pushing a three-wheeled handcart. On all the basement railings down the road hung miniature pewter pots which he filled as he went whistling on his way. Outwardly all these vessels were gleaming and shining, but I wonder how aseptic were their interiors?

The milkman and his pewter pots seemed innocent enough to me as a child, but I thought of drains as an all-pervading menace, a destroying force moving underground. Iron grills swallowed the rainwater as it flowed along the gutters, thirsty monsters belching forth sickness and death. I recall grown-ups shaking their heads. 'I thought I noticed a strange smell, dear. Did you have the drains checked before you bought the house?'

2

I must have been nearly seven when we left London and went to live in Wimbledon. The move was a natural one for us. Wimbledon was considered a stockbroker's paradise. It had the further attraction that my mother's younger sister, Lily Hamilton, lived there with her elderly husband and two grown stepchildren. And, finally, it was a wonderful place to be a child.

We lived on the Ridgeway near the Common. Up the Lauriston Road and there you were among heather and bracken, ponds and lakes, a golf course, an old windmill and Roman remains known as Caesar's Camp. Acres and acres of green grass, copses and dells, and the seasonal beauty of oak and birch against a skyline without the limitations of a London park.

Our house, 'Ebisham', was a rather pretentious red brick building with gables and a glassed-in porch. One entered into a square hall with a gallery overhead, off which the nursery and our bedrooms opened. On the rare occasions when our parents gave a dinner party or a dance, we would creep out of bed to look down from between the banisters on the wonderful world of grown-ups. A world full of secrets; exciting secrets we were growing towards inch by slow inch, as shown by Nanny's pencil marks on the nursery door. 'Oh, God, let me grow up quickly' – a half-whispered prayer drowned by the buzz of adult talk and laughter.

We children had more of a social life than in London. Some of the children we got to know went to convent day schools, and so there were birthday parties and tea parties and more than one Christmas party with trees laden with presents, crackers to pull, and flickering candles clipped to the branches, showing up the beauty of the spun glass ornaments. There were big houses all round the Common, and the people who lived in them had money to spend.

Cuthbert and I were taken to Mass on Sundays at the

Catholic Church on Edgehill. It was only ten minutes walk away and had a large, prosperous and socially active congregation. My mother, as the wife of a stockbroker and mindful of possible clients, did her duty and launched herself into this circle of activities. And so it was that she met Richard Austin Freeman, the young doctor whose practice was building up in the skilful hands of the Jesuit fathers of Edgehill.

'A very able man. Tragic his having to leave the Colonial Service. Oh yes, blackwater fever – he was invalided out.'

So now he was practising medicine in Wimbledon, having been forced by illness to give up a successful career as Assistant Colonial Surgeon in West Africa. He had not yet begun to publish the scientific detective stories that would one day make him famous.

At this time my mother was expecting her fourth child, so they met, initially, as doctor and patient. Her new Catholic friends assured her that she had made a wise choice in the matter of her physician: 'My dear, quite hypnotic. Just looks at you and you feel he knows everything.' He was a striking-looking man. I remember as a child wondering whether his dark, mesmeric eyes could look right through me. The thought frightened me slightly, and the idea that he could probably read the thoughts buzzing round in my head was even more disturbing. He would make jokes when he came to see us, but we never seemed able to share them with him as we shared the jokes of Cook's friend, the milkman.

My third brother, Gerald, was born that winter. In those days a lady had her own midwife, booked weeks before the interesting event. She took over the mother-to-be ten days or so before the infant was due to arrive. We children liked our mother's midwife, Mrs Hopkins (a courtesy title – I'm sure there was never a Mr Hopkins). She was short, stout, and jolly, with twinkling eyes behind thick-lensed glasses. It seemed to us she must be on quite friendly terms with the Royal Family, for one of her favourite lines was 'As the Queen does at Windsor'. She would pick up a chicken bone from her plate and, before our scandalized eyes, nibble at it with her clicking false teeth, saying as she did so, 'As the Queen does at Windsor'. We knew her teeth were false because she sometimes took them out and laid them on the table. This habit, we gathered, was also shared by Her Majesty. Mrs Hopkins had lots of real-life anecdotes to tell, but many of them were not for our ears. She and Nanny would sit by the dying fire in the evenings, and their whispers tickled our ears with a sense of hidden drama.

We came in from our walk one morning just after Christmas, our cheeks pink, our eyes shining. Nanny had taken us to the pond at the end of the road. Cuthbert and I had been out on the ice, sliding and shouting, while Nanny walked Carteret, the toddler, round and round the frozen circle, holding the reins that kept him happy as a make-believe horse: 'Gee-up, Nanny, gee-up.' Round and round, till she decided that enough was enough and marched us home. At home, Mrs Hopkins' portentous figure came down the stairs to greet us:

'And what do you think I've just found under a gooseberry bush in the garden?'

Cuthbert, who had a literal mind, ventured, 'A gooseberry?'

'No, no, Master Cuthbert. A new baby brother for you. What do you think of that?'

'I like goosegogs,' said Carteret, with the one-track mind of a four-year-old.

But Nanny's rather wooden face was beaming. 'All well, Nellie?' she asked. 'The mistress not too shook up?'

'No, no. The fourth – like shelling peas.'

As I went to sleep that night my mind was twisting this assurance round and round. What had that remark about shelling peas got to do with my mother? And why should she be 'shook up'? And how could a new baby be picked from under a gooseberry bush?

We had a tabby in those days called Miau Puss Cat. She was a kitchen cat that slept in a box near the big black stove and was never allowed in any other part of the house. She earned her board and lodging by catching mice. We loved her, and, on Cook's day out, when we had tea in the kitchen, we lay on the floor watching, fascinated, as Miau Puss Cat lapped milk from a saucer, her pink tongue like a spoon, scooping it up. Lovely days! Sarah, the house-parlourmaid always made us dripping toast as a treat.

But, alas, Miau Puss Cat had one great failing – she was forever producing kittens. While we had one on our hands, we were allowed to play with it in the nursery. I never cared for dolls, but all our female relations thought I should, so they gave me dolls in all shapes and sizes, and a doll's house, and a cradle,

23

and, best of all, a pram. And Nanny, being the soft-hearted creature she was, allowed me to wheel out the current kitten in the doll's pram, to the envy of all the other little girls. Cook and the milkman, in collusion, did their best to find good homes for these unwanted offspring, but at last the list of good homes needing kittens had to be written off.

Then, one afternoon, we children came home with Nanny to find Dr Freeman on his way out, leaving a queer, sickly smell behind him. And our mother was there in the hall saying, 'Thank you, Dick, it was very good of you.'

Thanking him for what? There was Cook in the kitchen, her face all streaked with tears. Of course we never saw Miau Puss Cat again and about this time, I think, the first whisper of a scandal must have started. In those days you could not be on first name terms with your doctor and not expect to start the grass whispering.

Cook, while we were in Wimbledon, was a tall, gaunt, Yorkshire-woman, called Eva. She was being courted by a widower known to us as Mr Nicholls, who had a small hardware shop in New Cross. On her day off, Eva, presumably, travelled to New Cross. But on most Sunday evenings, Mr Nicholls was to be found in our kitchen. My mother did not approve of the 'no followers allowed' rule often insisted upon for women servants. The visits of Eva's paunchy suitor were a source of great excitement in the nursery, for he brought us fascinating offerings from his shop – tiny sample pots of paint were especially prized.

As a great honour I was invited to sit on his knee while he and Eva exchanged remarks over my head. She was always telling him, 'Give over, Albert, you should know better than to say such things before the young lady. Yonder is the door and out you go if you don't give over.'

Poor Eva was a periodic alcoholic. I remember coming in from our walk one day, and there she was lying under the kitchen table. 'Nanny,' we exclaimed, staring open-mouthed, 'why has Cook gone to bed in the kitchen?' Eva's period of service ended with her marriage from our parents' house. She was an orphan and most of the wedding guests, therefore, were friends or relations of the bridegroom. They all had loud voices and louder laughs. The best man was almost as good as a clown, we decided, with a big white carnation in his buttonhole and a seemingly endless stock of jokes, some of which, fortunately perhaps, were incomprehensible to us. But there were plenty we could share in, and when it came to tying an old boot on to the back of the 'fly' which was to take the happy couple to the station, we were thrilled to be taken on as collaborators.

Eva was something more than a good plain cook and her last service to my mother was to make three Christmas puddings: one for Christmas day, one for New Year's Day, and one for Easter. There was a ritual about this. On the evening before the stir-about, Eva put the mixture into shining white basins. The next evening we all went down to the kitchen, where Eva, High Priestess in a white apron and white cap, stood poised with wooden spoon in hand before a big bowl. My father carried in a small bottle of brandy, which he duly poured into the gooey and delicious smelling concoction. Then Eva handed him the spoon, and he stirred the spicy mess. The spoon was handed from one to the other of us for a stir, so that a year's luck was assured. That evening I unwittingly contributed more than a lucky wish. For on Christmas Day, instead of the ring, or the thimble, or the sixpence, my father found a child's tooth in his helping.

I remember two major events while we were in Wimbledon. Even Nanny would not miss the military manoeuvres on the Common – red coats and cannon, the mock battles and galloping horses, and words of command that cracked out like pistol shots and were obeyed on the instant. The whole of the Common seemed to erupt into volcanic movement, while the usual dog-walking ladies peeped out from behind lace curtains. Days later we picked up valuable souvenirs in the shape of empty cartridge cases.

The other event was a circus that pitched its tent on the wide open spaces. If we were lucky, we met the procession of animals parading through the town and up into the village, where the elite lived. There were two elephants, a disdainful-looking camel, and, best of all, little piebald ponies. Also, of course, there was the beautiful white horse, straight out of Grimm's fairy tales, with nodding plumes on its head and a fairy princess on its back. Father took us to the circus; I think secretly he enjoyed it himself. We preferred a circus to a pantomime because of the animals. To see the slinky, terrifying tigers, the awe-inspiring lions leaping from block to block and posing on the top of the steps at the crack of a whip chilled and thrilled our barbarous little egos. On the occasion of my first circus there was a grand finale of Cowboys and Indians, with rifle shots echoing round the big marquee. This sent me tumbling down from our select balcony seats; running, running, into the arms of a fat lady selling oranges just outside the tent.

'Here, lovely,' she comforted, 'don't take on so. Them's only make-believe shootin's and killin's.' And, as my father appeared, she grabbed me by the arm and thrust an orange into my hand. 'Now, dearie, who would want to harm a pretty little thing like you.'

My first experience of real violence, of any kind, was quite different. One day I was sent out to post a letter in the box near our house. I pushed it in and had turned to walk back when, suddenly, from nowhere, a girl rather older than myself hurled herself at me and shook me violently by the shoulders, speaking no word. And I think, perhaps, that the silence was the most frightening part of the attack. Then, as suddenly as she had appeared, she vanished. I had never seen her before – I never saw her again. Tears sprang to my eyes. I felt humiliated as well as frightened. 'Why? Why?' I asked myself. But I never told anyone. A strange little incident, odd and unrelated, but etched forever on my mind.

3

Family holidays were a great institution in those days. People taking lodgings by the seaside were a source of income for retired butlers who had married the cook. It was as much a partnership as a marriage. With their mutual savings they would buy a sizeable house and, living in the basement themselves, would rent the upper floors 'with service'. Satisfied clients often booked rooms from season to season.

Nanny had a cousin Emma, a widow, who let such lodgings in Westgate-on-Sea. Spending the summer holidays with Emma was like going from one home to another. Her house was about ten minutes walk from the seafront, in a quiet square. If we were lucky, we were given the rooms that opened on to a balcony overlooking the square garden.

We travelled by train in a second-class carriage reserved for us. The guard, touching his peaked cap deferentially, locked us in against the less lucky travelling public, and, indeed, we took up most of the carriage with our cases, a hamper for bed linen, and a basket which imprisoned the family cat, who mewed piteously and had to be let out for brief spells of comforting. It was not a long journey even by the standards of the old South Eastern and Chatham railway, and we enjoyed every minute of it.

We were allowed to lower the window and stick our heads out to watch when the train stopped for the engine to take a 'drink of water' and the stoker hopped down from the cab to attach the great hose-pipe. Otherwise, the windows were kept shut because of smuts and possible grit in one's eye. But the smoke in the tunnels was so acrid and sulphurous that it penetrated even the closed windows, and at these times Nanny always covered the baby's mouth with a handkerchief. Tunnels were dark and delightfully frightening, like the caves in cliffs that might hide an ogre or a cloud of bats.

When we reached our destination, Nanny and the baby were

27

packed with the luggage into the station fly while we elder ones went with our mother. Hop, skip and jumping (the decorum proper for a London street was not necessary for Westgate), we reached Emma's house.

And there she was, a plump little woman with white hair, pink cheeks, and blue eyes that smiled a welcome. And Alice, her daughter, stood beside her, a tall, gawky girl smiling and giving practical help with hats and coats and parcels. Mother and daughter – a tall, slim birch tree beside a cosy little rose bush covered with pale, sweet pink roses.

It was Alice who brought us tea when dusk fell over Ethelbert Square and we were settled in our holiday home. There was jam and cake and a big plate of bread and butter gathered round an imposing silver-plated cruet, which held bottles of sauces and swivelled round on its base at the touch of a finger – when Nanny was not looking, we gave it that touch. But the peak of pleasure was the fact that Alice always gave us an 'egg to our tea' that first evening. For some reason this boiled egg 'to our tea' capped the delights of the journey that started when the guard waved his green flag and blew his whistle and we chugged and puffed our way to the seaside.

Father came to join us for long weekends, but he was not really a part of our holiday; and, indeed, Mother also was only a part-time visitor.

Westgate-on-Sea was a very select resort. The gorgeous vulgarity of minstrels, coconut shies and donkey rides on the sands were not permitted. They would not have been a practical proposition in any case, for at high tide the sands were completely covered and the sea washed up against the concrete of the seafront.

If you wanted that sort of thing you had to go to Margate where the lovely golden sands were never wholly covered. But you had to persuade a grown-up to take you there in the horse-drawn tram, and the tram lines stopped short of the town. Genteel and select, that was how its residents wished to keep Westgate. Metaphorically, she drew her skirts aside from the vulgarity of her sister town.

Margate, though, had every kind of excitement: a pier with penny-in-the-slot machines; donkeys waiting patiently for the children, who, for twopence, could ride all along the firm wet sand at the water's edge, while a small boy ran beside, whacking at the donkey's rump with a stick. There were also goat carriages up on the seafront for the younger children, who held the reins in their podgy hands and urged on the shaggy animal with cries of 'Gee-up, goat'. But it was the minstrels with their blackened faces and rollicking songs we liked best of all. They had a way of making the audience a part of the show, picking out a boy or girl here and there to recite a poem or pipe out a song and giving a bag of sweets for a prize.

There were always a lot of people on the beach. At low tide we watched the bathing machines being drawn down into the distant sea by a patient old horse. They were like big wooden dog kennels on wheels, with a door at the back and little steps so that you could walk right into the water. Many of the men bathers would swim out into the deeper water, but the ladies, on that part of the beach allotted to them, usually contented themselves with jumping up and down in the waves, never getting the big mob caps on their heads wet. Both sexes dressed in suits that buttoned up to the neck in front, and women's suits were skirted. No sunbathing then, no gleaming torsos lying on towels, like bodies dropped from outer space. No – having had your dip you got straight into your dark and dank-smelling machine and dressed right away.

We, ourselves, were allowed to take off our shoes and stockings, as bathing and paddling were considered strengthening for the constitution. My skirts had to be pinned round my waist.

If we were lucky our visits to Margate would coincide with the arrival of the daily pleasure steamer, the *Southend Belle*, a paddle boat that churned its slow way to Southend, just below the estuary of the Thames, to Margate. We were envious of the motley crowd that came down the gangway waving streamers and beer bottles in a real holiday mood.

Yet Westgate had its own quiet attractions. Its possibilities were controlled by the tide, but this did not trouble us. Red and white valerian, scarlet poppies and great clumps of feathery green fennel grew on the chalky headland. Emma would occasionally ask us to pick some of the fennel for her and then she would make a delicious aromatic sauce to pour over the mackerel she boiled in her shining copper kettle. We sailed kites at the top of the cliffs or went fishing for crabs when the tide was in. Bait was supplied by Emma's friendly fishmonger.

He would take off his straw hat and bow to me.

'What can I do for you today, Madam?'

'Please, Mr Jones, will you give us some fishes' heads?'

'Certainly, Madam', he would say with a wink as he replaced his hat and deposited half a dozen of these revolting castoffs into Cuthbert's little tin bucket.

Then off we went with Nanny to the cove beneath the cliffs where the waves were lapping against the walls and break-waters. We tied lengths of string to our bait, and, lying on our tummies, lowered the lines into the water. We could see the small green shore crabs, dim shapes, digging their claws into the bait. Then, slowly, with breathless care, we pulled up our lines. The lucky ones fell off, but the unlucky ones clung on, and we pulled them up and off and dropped them into our bucket. Nanny saw to it that we eventually returned them to their seaweed home.

Nanny, in her way, must have been just as unconventional in her attitude to our upbringing as was our mother. I cannot imagine any of her London colleagues allowing us to do some of the things she did. But she was never off-guard, never burying her head in a book or becoming absorbed in a conversation; she was silently aware of us and protecting us all the time. Most of a child's heart was given to the nannies of those days, a wonderful band of women whose selfless devotion meant security and love.

We had a friend who sometimes shared our holidays, the son of my mother's dearest friend, Lily Mason, and her husband Frank, who seemed to be the constant beneficiaries of inherit-ances from various relatives. They would go off to Italy or some other faraway spot, and while they were gone, Frankie would float from one of his parents' friends to another.

Nanny made no secret of her mistrust of Frankie Mason. 'Upsetting, that's what he is,' she would mutter. 'And it's never him that's to blame, oh, no!' she added with heavy sarcasm. There was, for example, the day he incited us to throw rocks on to the middle of the road, and when Nanny and the pram caught up with us, we were being taken to task by an irate old gentleman, but Frankie, the instigator, had vanished. Secretly we admired his daring, although we suffered the consequences.

One day Frankie and I were down on the beach poking about

in the rock pools, collecting winkles for our tea, when he whispered to me, 'Come on, let's walk to Margate while the tide's out. Nanny is making sand castles with the little brats; no-one will notice.'

I hesitated for a moment – then my more reckless self took over. 'Let's,' I said.

He was right, no-one did notice. But halfway there I got scared. The tide was coming in. Shining pool was linking up with shining pool; the sea was moving towards us, gentle but relentless. I thought of King Canute; I thought of Mary, the girl who was drowned when she went to call the cattle home across the sands of Dee, and I became so scared that I wet my knickers. Crimson in the face I struggled on, fear of the sea now accentuated by fear that my shameful lapse would be discovered. Suddenly I saw a way out of both predicaments. Edging towards the oncoming waves, I staged a stumble and fell into the water. My two problems were solved. 'Frankie,' I gasped, picking myself up. 'I'm soaking wet, I'll catch my death.' And, without waiting for a reply, I started running back, life and honour saved.

Even on rainy days at Emma's we were never at a loss for an occupation and amusement. Nanny, being a cousin, was a privileged person, and this extended to us. Nanny and Emma would sit by the stove in the kitchen, and we were allowed to use the snuggery across the passage as our workshop. On a round table covered by oilcloth we played card games (beggar-my-neighbour was our favourite) or worked at our special crafts, inspired by treasures picked up on the shore. Holding a piece of cardboard under water, we would tease out a frond of feathery seaweed with a pin, and when it dried on the card we would set it aside to be used as a Christmas gift, suitably inscribed. Given a pot of glue, some small empty boxes and a dish of silvery sand, we made what we considered to be wonderful presents out of the shells we had collected: tiny cowries, round yellow winkles, and many more. We also did 'Berlin wool work', a sort of coarse cross-stitch on canvas. Our patience and ambition seldom ventured beyond the creation of small square kettle holders. These were lined by Nanny, until she decided it was time I learned to sew.

We shared all these activities, for whilst our contemporaries went to boarding schools, we were given lessons at home and

31

had little or no contact at any time with other children. The upper-middle-class parent of that day had to choose between home education by a governess or tutor, boarding schools, or small private day schools, sometimes called academies, where the staff were often quite unqualified. The state schools were called Board schools, and were not even to be considered. They were for the 'lower classes', and if any subjects other than the basic three 'R's' were suggested for their curriculum, hands were raised in horror that these working-class children would be given ideas above their station.

When we went on holiday, it was usually to Emma's; and when we went to London, it was almost always to Grandfather's house in Prince of Wales Terrace. Grandfather, founder and head of the firm in which my father was a 'reluctant stock-broker', was a fierce little man, whose red face contrasted rather harshly with his white hair and beard. A Santa Claus without jollity. We were scared of him, even when he patted us on the head and bestowed a half-crown tip on us.

He was a widower for many years, and our Aunt Florence ran his house until his second marriage to Maria O'Connor-Morris. I have often wondered why this charming, cultured lady married the pompous little stockbroker. Probably it was a marriage of convenience. He was, at that time, a wealthy man; she had no money, but she had a circle of rich, famous and influential friends: Mrs La Touche of Harristown, the banker's wife, John Ruskin, Aubrey de Vere, Coventry Patmore, Laurence Housman, and many others. The house in Prince of Wales Terrace, Kensington, became an active 'cell' of culture.

According to our mother, Aunt Florence blossomed into colourful fulfilment with the activity brought about by her father's new wife. I sometimes think that the emotional reason behind this marriage of apparent incompatibles was that Maria O'Connor-Morris got herself a daughter who, in the language of the day, 'worshipped the ground she trod on'.

But all this is second-hand knowledge, built up with what my mother told us long afterwards. Our parents went to some of the dinner parties there, but they were never really in that inner circle. My aunt and Mother had personalities that clashed. I think they both struggled to suppress their dislike of each other, but every now and then it erupted. One constant source of irritation was my mother's growing friendship with Richard Austin Freeman, whom Aunt Florence considered 'not even a gentleman'.

Our Aunt Florence was good to us in her way, but it had to be her way. However, she had a personal maid called Timmins, whom we really loved. Timmins, a warm-hearted Irishwoman, spoiled us. She would creep into our bedroom with titbits from the dinner table and whisper, 'I don't know what your aunt would say, Miss Dorothy. Don't make any crumbs for the love of blessed Mary, or it's meself will be off to dear old Ireland in the mornin'.'

We were allowed the freedom of the house after our grandfather had left for the City, but after we got back from our afternoon walk Nanny kept us out of the way upstairs. Once, bored with this arrangement, and greatly daring, I sneaked down to do a bit of spying. The dining room door was open and I could see Jeynes, the butler, setting the table. And – was it possible? – my aunt was lending a hand, clad only in petticoat and camisole. My eyes nearly popped out of my head with scandalized disbelief. But she was a supreme snob and, like all snobs, considered herself a person who socially could do no wrong.

When we grew older we paid individual visits to Kensington when Aunt Florence was there and were always given a treat of some kind. I shall always remember to her credit that it was she who gave me my first ride in a hansom cab. She was taking me to the pantomime in Drury Lane. So Jeynes, picking up the whistle kept on the hall table for that purpose, summoned a hansom cab. When it drew up to the kerb, Jeynes opened the wooden apron and I climbed in after my aunt. We pulled the rug provided over our knees and away we went, the invisible driver perched high on his little seat behind us. Every now and then we would see the long whip snaking out to touch the horse lightly on its flank. I have quite forgotten the glittering pantomime story but that ride remains as a wish fulfilled. Very occasionally Aunt Florence would take us to the shops in the High Street. She was well known at Barker's, for she was a fussy and exacting shopper. She would sit on the high stool in the glove department, her elbow resting on the velvet cushion placed on the counter for that purpose, and try on one pair after another. The girl behind the counter, gently pulling them on to the outstretched fingers, earned every penny of her meagre salary.

Our grandfather's house was also where we were sent when any of us went down with mumps or measles; a place of quarantine. After his remarriage and out of 'the Season' the house was deserted, for he had another house in Tunbridge Wells which his wife much preferred. So, when Cuthbert caused a sensation in the family by getting scarlet fever (something to be reckoned with in those days), we others were sent off to Prince of Wales Terrace.

Before we left, sheets were put into a bath filled with a solution of carbolic, wrung out, and hung up before his door. As Nanny hastily packed clothes, we asked, with a child's brutal frankness, 'Will he die, Nanny?'

For most children death is a remote contingency. You find a dead sparrow out on the lawn, perhaps, or come down to breakfast one morning to see one of the goldfish floating motionless on top of the water. People die discreetly, behind screens, as it were; somebody you know disappears out of your life – grown-ups protect you from the actual happening.

I remember very vividly the day I first saw death take over from life. I had to go to the dentist in Kensington, so my father brought me up to Prince of Wales Terrace to spend a couple of days. My aunt was very fond of her baby brother, whom she called 'dear Bernie', and so she was ready to help out on this sort of occasion.

On the second day I was turned over to Timmins. We had gone to Swan and Edgar's in Piccadilly Circus, to match some colour in a silk dress that Timmins was altering for my aunt, and we were to feed the ducks in St James's Park on the way home. We finished our errand and were starting to walk back, when we saw it happen.

Now the hill from Hyde Park to the Circus is much steeper than most people realize. Halfway down we decided to cross the road. A bus was pulling slowly up the hill, and just before it reached us, the near horse stumbled and fell. For two or three minutes its legs thrashed wildly in the air. And then it lay quite still. The summer sun shone on its sweating body. It was dead. The driver got down from his seat; the passengers all alighted, talking and exclaiming. I gripped Timmins by the arms, 'Oh is it really dead?'

34

'It is, love, it is,' soothed Timmins. 'But perhaps it's better dead. It's a hard, hard life for them poor animals, so it is.' And she led me away to sunlit St James's Park.

Our stepgrandmother died while we were still young. Though she never entered our lives to any great extent, she became a legend, a dim but golden image in my memory, remembered best in the setting of one summer holiday spent in Tunbridge Wells. Our parents had rented a small, semi-detached house in a street of similar, nondescript semi-detached houses. The reason for this break from our usual holiday by the sea I have long since forgotten, if I ever knew it. But we enjoyed every minute of every day.

Tunbridge Wells was a well-known spa where people came to drink the waters, yellow from their iron content, and to gather in the fashionable shops of the Pantiles. But for us the rocky outcrops on the nearby common were a far greater attraction. We never tired of scrambling about on the craggy surfaces of Toad Rock and Pulpit Rock – names fit for a child's paradise. Shrubberies to hide in, fat gooseberries to be picked warily from spiky bushes. 'Here's the church and here's the steeple and out come all the holy people,' we chanted as we squeezed the great hairy yellow berries. But best of all were the little Alpine strawberries that grew by the front gate.

Tea was served on the lawn under the shade of the trees. Our Aunt Florence was like a Dresden china figurine, silver hair piled high on her head, a chiffon bow perched like a gay butterfly on top; her neat little person trim in a suit of white linen or tussore silk, pouring tea from a silver teapot into delicate china cups. Meanwhile, Maria O'Connor-Morris, in her wheelchair, beamed on us all. She was now a semi-invalid who could no longer journey to and fro, but her friends gathered round her, a cosmopolitan crowd of intellectuals. She loved my mother, whose intellect matched her own, and I think the antagonism between my mother and Aunt Florence may originally have been sparked off by jealousy over the attention of this remarkable woman.

I can see her now, a studio portrait study of a grey-haired lady, gossamer-knit Shetland shawl drawn over her thin shoulders as she sat in her wheelchair, her ebony stick with its chased silver handle lying beside her on the grass.

Looking back I realize how kaleidoscopic was the pattern of

35

our life. We were not an ordinary rooted family living in the same house year after year, meeting the same neighbourhood people day after day. Our education was not divided into school terms and holidays. A great variety of personalities came and went in our circle. They looked in, departed, returned or disappeared for ever. Our contacts with other children were rare – artificial contacts at parties, on the beach, chance meetings in the park, where we hardly got past the preliminary staring and assessing stage. And we had no young cousins nearby. I suppose Frankie, the evil genie in our lives, was our nearest experience of friendship.

But we were never dull. The normal joining in and sharing of games and organized activities being denied us, we found our own interests, which were many and varied. We lived in an adult world with which we had no real communication, yet we did not seem to suffer for it. We were pawns set down here and there, but we never felt insecure, for there was always Nanny. And where she was, we found security, even after the real nursery days were over.

4

Our next move was to Gravesend. It was an important town, though architecturally quite unimpressive. Built at the estuary of the Thames, it was the gateway to the capital. The Port of London Authority had its headquarters there. A moored barge, named the *Hygeia*, housed the health officers, and they had a quarantine hospital on the river bank. The Customs and Excise people would board the great liners before the river pilots in their fussy little tugs towed them into the berths at Tilbury Docks on the opposite shore. Gravesend was also a garrison town, but, unlike Wimbledon, it was a social dead end, and officers of the regiment unlucky enough to be stationed there thought of it as exile and were aggrieved.

Why we moved we children never knew, but I think our combined guess was right; the move to Gravesend was in some way connected with the Freeman family. When we left Wimbledon the Freemans had also left, and temporarily, they dropped out of our world, though our parents must have known their whereabouts. My suspicion is that there was something of a scandal in Wimbledon over Richard Austin Freeman's relationship with my mother, and that would have meant the end of the medical practice he was building there.

At about this time, Richard took chambers in Clifford's Inn and got down to the business of writing. Then, at intervals, he paid visits to our house. Gravesend is not far from London, and I seem to recall that tickets were cheap; indeed, a second-class return cost around half-a-crown. So our mother, now an indispensable part of his life, spent her time commuting between Clifford's Inn and our house in Constitution Crescent – helping, advising and, later, typing his work on her portable Blick. As his books rolled out of the printing presses, they corrected proofs together.

If you have read his books you will have noted that his heroines are all of one type, and I believe that they are a record

37

of how he saw our mother. They are 'handsome' and intelligent, but with no sense of fun, no inconsistencies, no passion. Not our mother as we knew her, but probably the woman he saw mirrored in his precise and formal mind.

We accepted him – we had to – but we were aloof and a little resentful, for as soon as he appeared, our mother's attention was drawn away from us and from our activities. Day after day, it seemed, Cook was told to make sandwiches, and off they went – the collaborators – for long sessions in the lovely Kentish countryside: Cobham, Cobham Woods, the marshes at Hoo. They sometimes took my mother's tricycle, riding and walking in turns. A strange couple in many ways. Did Richard love my mother? Or did he look on her as a promoter, content to stay in the background? Was her belief in him a part of his inspiration, a driving force? Nanny never said anything. I always felt that there was a very special relationship between her and my mother, a relationship that even the wedge of Richard Austin Freeman could not split. But she never beamed on him as she did on other guests; the wooden face remained wooden.

I was nine years old now and no longer finding the sole companionship of younger brothers satisfying enough for my expanding mind. I turned to the world of books, and found communication with the friends created there, identifying myself with the heroines in a most satisfying way. My taste in literature was catholic. As well as Dickens, Kipling and Sir Walter Scott, I eagerly devoured a magazine entitled *The Churchman's Companion*, to which Nanny subscribed. There was one serial I followed with breathless interest. The heroine was a young woman called Alice, an artisan's wife, who was a model manager and housekeeper. I cannot imagine what I found so thrilling in Alice's economies and contrivances to make ends meet and keep her husband happy. But the workings of a child's mind are unpredictable, and I owe many happy hours to Nanny's *Churchman's Companion*.

Then a major crisis occurred that brought us into intimate contact with the Freeman family. Richard was paying our parents one of his periodic visits when he became suddenly and gravely ill. Perhaps this illness was somehow connected to the blackwater fever he had contracted during his service in Africa. In any case, consultations followed panic, and we were told that

Nanny would take Gerald and Carteret to her cousin in Tunbridge Wells and that Cuthbert and I were to stay with Auntie Austin Freeman in Ramsgate.

The decision was like a dark cloud looming up from some totally unexpected quarter. That night, as we lay in the darkness, fear and apprehension were menacing shapes hovering over us. Even the night-light, glimmering in its saucer of water, could not bring the reassurance it usually did. Was it the end of the world? Daylight had not long taken over when Nanny woke us and hurried us into our clothes, shaking her head as we plied her with questions. Then she relented, as she spooned the porridge into our plates. 'You and Master Cuthbert will like Ramsgate,' she told us. 'It has a pier and lovely sands.'

'What about you?' we asked. The thought of Ramsgate without her did not console us at all.

'Oh, we'll be all right with Nellie, and it won't be for long,' she told us. But we noticed the tears trickling down her weathered cheeks.

Long, long before we got to Annie Austin's dull little villa in Ramsgate, I was aware of the gnawing pangs of homesickness. The housemaid took us there, a bony, sallow-faced girl, who more than once had reported us to Nanny for stealing lumps of sugar out of the silver bowl she kept in the pantry. Telling tales, we informed her, was worse than stealing sugar in the scale of misdeeds. But this unexpected break from dull routine had put her in a good mood, and she actually bought us each a barley sugar stick to suck on the journey. To Cuthbert's indignation, she insisted on getting into a 'Ladies Only' compartment. Nanny, she said, had told her to do this, and we knew that Nanny regarded all strange men as criminals and molesters of innocent women.

Richard's wife, warned by telegram, was waiting for us on the platform at Ramsgate with her two boys. In the Wimbledon days there had been no social intercourse between us and the Freeman family: we did not know them, but we knew of them. Annie was a dumpy little woman, not unlike Noah's wife as imagined by the toymakers. Jack, the older boy, was a little younger than Cuthbert and pompous as an old man; Laurence, the younger, was a replica of his mother and a real little skirt-hanger. They were an odd couple, and children distrust anyone or anything out of the ordinary. We ignored them as being

39

totally without interest, and listened to our elders as our bodyguard handed us over, with an explanatory letter, and gave her own highly coloured version of the past twenty-four hours.

That exile was heavy going. We liked Annie Austin, as we called her behind her back. She was pompous and her speech was stilted, but there was a sort of formal kindliness about her. She would make batches of a sweet called coconut ice – pink and white bars of a delicious chewiness – for our benefit, and home-made lemonade was pressed upon us when other people would have offered water from the tap. Annie Austin did her best, but a homesick child is not an easy problem to tackle. We felt lost and imprisoned in her prim little house with its atmosphere of cabbage water and soap suds.

Even the furniture was a source of depression. Dull red plush covered chairs in what Annie referred to as the 'parlour'. The mantelpiece was a shelf for souvenirs, mostly china trifles from every seaside resort in England. Red wool bobbles edged the plush runner on which they stood. The wallpaper was an indeterminate green. If it was a sunny day, Annie pulled the pink velvet curtains across the window to save the too-bright red carpet from fading. She explained that the house was rented, and she felt she had to take extra care. She bustled in one day to tell me this, because I had pulled the curtains aside to watch a girls' school out walking, two by two, in what was called a crocodile. The chattering, laughing girls made me feel even lonelier in my self-pity.

Meanwhile, my mother and Richard Freeman's colleagues from the Middlesex Hospital were fighting hard to save his life. They succeeded, and by doing so, gave Dr Thorndyke, the principal character of his subsequent scientific detective stories, to the world of fiction. We returned home to find a gaunt and shaky edition of our parents' guest looking as if he had returned from the grave. The dark, aquiline good looks, the magnetic fire of the dark eyes, were changed and dimmed by the ordeal of a desperate sickness.

Constitution Crescent was built on a hill. There were only five tall houses out of the dozen or so planned – the beginning of a bankrupt builder's dream. At the very top of the house were three rooms: the servants' bedroom, my father's darkroom (for he was now a dedicated photographer), and the so-called study.

40

Here, two platforms had been built, one under each window. And on each platform a telescope was mounted.

The view up and down the river was magnificent. The telescopes reached out and brought all the wonder of the river into one small room. I suspect that the idea of that lookout was instigated by Richard Freeman. He and my mother spent many hours looking over the estuary, studying the vessels that moved up and down, the brigs and brigantines, the schooners and barques, the barges (river vessels, children of the Thames, these) with their red-brown sails and blunt bows lying low in the water, weighed down by their cargoes of coal and the like, and then the busy little tugs and occasional big liners – a floating world of wealth and adventure. The sailing ships lying at anchor, sails furled, looked like lovely skeletons. But they were lovelier still in full sail – mainsail and topsail, jib and flying jib, bellying in the wind as they set off on their endless voyaging.

Richard Freeman was a fanatical lover of ships. He knew all the rigs and all the details of every rig. He made models of ships, and his favourite pub was the Ship and Lobster, a drab little building on the edge of the marshland that stretched to the Hundreds of Hoo and beyond. It was the pub of the watermen, with whom he drank many a beer and shared many an anecdote. The two telescopes were a great help in his convalescence because, for a mind like his, activities of all kinds were a necessity. Condemned to inactivity of body, he was content to pause and dream and look through the telescopes that could bring his beloved river to him.

What did my mother think when she first looked at Richard Austin Freeman with her wide, intelligent grey eyes? Was there electricity in the air, the warning rumble of thunder? My conviction is that almost from the beginning she saw him as an extraordinary man, someone at whose feet she could sit, yet someone she could direct and dominate. Did they become lovers in the usual sense? Or was sex overruled, sublimated to the making of a new writer? I am quite sure she saw him as famous long before Fame arrived. I am almost equally sure that underneath his magnetic personality was a cold and calculating mind. For in my mother's hand was my father's cheque book. A strange eternal triangle.

And yet a partnership (let us acknowledge it) that enriched three lives, for in the end my father also basked in the reflected

41

fame of Richard Freeman. My father was a stockbroker. Did he, perhaps, look on Richard Freeman as a gilt-edged investment? It was not many years before he broke into the world of detective fiction, and in the first book to make his name, *The Red Thumb Mark*, my father's assistance in photographic experiments is acknowledged. But it was before all this that my father bought the house in Woodville Terrace, Gravesend, into which the Freemans moved and settled. Ironically, it was the house in which my father himself was born.

The arrangement was that Dr Freeman would provide free medical care and free education, as our tutor, in exchange for a roof for him and his family – and everyone's face was saved. As far as teaching sessions went, an hour or so a day was not an excessive amount of time by any calculation. Be that as it may, our education was, for the first time, definitely taken in hand. Shepherded by our mother, we three children walked down from Constitution Crescent to hear lectures on: physiology, biology, physical geography, physics and the steam engine, logic, and Egyptian history and hieroglyphics. Certainly a mixed bag.

We rang the bell at Number 2, Woodville Terrace, and the door was opened by Annie Austin in a flowered apron. 'Good morning, Mrs Freeman,' said my mother.

'Good morning, Mrs Bishop', was the reply. Never, never, did the two women come to first-name terms.

The room set aside for us was grandly called 'the classroom'. In it were a blackboard, half a dozen hard chairs, and an armchair for my mother. The one window was draped with yellow curtains – a colour favoured by Annie throughout the house. There was no carpet on the floor, but the floor boards were clean and scrubbed, and we knew who scrubbed them. The two Freeman boys were fellow pupils.

There was never any pressure on us during childhood; no exams, no competition, no rigid timetable. We grew up like the flowers of the field, unstaked, unpruned, and untied.

The lectures were very elementary, and we never seemed to come to grips with any of the subjects. Not even with physiology and biology, which a doctor might have been expected to enlarge upon. Sex and the reproductive organs were more or less brushed under the carpet. In some ways Richard Freeman was very Victorian – prim and proper – and our mother was present at these lectures. Parents in that day and age of taboos were very tight-lipped about such things. Illness was also a taboo subject. You were told never to enquire what was the matter with anyone who was ill; I imagine because it might concern some portion of the human anatomy too indelicate to mention.

On my tenth birthday, it was decided that I learn to play the piano. I showed no special interest in music, and had no wish to be taught to play that instrument. But it was expected of a girl in those days to have at least some elementary training in voice and piano, especially piano. A Mrs King took me in hand. She was a small woman whose feet barely reached the pedals. She wore frilly dresses and left a trail of cheap scent behind her. I was fascinated by the rings on her fingers, winking and twinkling as she played over the piece I was to study. I was supposed to practise on our piano for half an hour every day, but Czerny's five-finger exercises killed any latent feeling I might have had for music.

If my musical education was a washout, I now developed another interest – writing. Since the age of eight I had read everything I could lay my hands on, stumbling over the longer words, and coming up with some odd mispronunciations. I started with poetry, always a beginner's stand-by, and I still have a booklet of collected verses, printed by Richard Freeman's brother, Bob, who had a small printing business. The Freeman brothers were also enthusiastic landscape painters, and Bob sometimes appeared with his painting gear to take Richard out for the day. Our house became, in time, a Freeman gallery. But I digress. Kipling's *Barrack Room Ballads* was one of my favourite books at this time, and 'They're Hangin' Danny Deever in the Mornin'' filled me with a sort of ghoulish enjoyment. My first poems were all sorrowful.

I also decided to edit and publish a magazine to be called *The Children's Sun*; however, I soon met with labour troubles – the boys refused to cooperate. Undeterred, I wrote the first instalment of a serial, made up a riddle ('solution promised in our next issue'), and wrote an article on toffee making. Then, of course, there must be a Court Circular, as there was in my father's paper. Our pet hedgehog having recently died, I wrote his obituary. I managed to squeeze a penny from each reluctant subscriber for a read of the magazine but, not surprisingly, only one issue appeared.

My efforts as a writer of plays were more successful, and the fun of dressing-up helped. Rehearsals, however, were hard going. Nanny, behind a draped clotheshorse, was prompter, and her voice was heard a lot more often than those of the work-shy actors. In one production my white rat, Nefertari (for we were getting into Egyptian history then), created a sensation. She was being transformed into a handsome prince (Cuthbert in outgrown velvet suit and lace collar), when she escaped amongst the audience. Annie Austin pushed her out of the room in a panic, calling on 'Richard' to help her; he was never 'Dick' to her, as he was to my mother.

Now that the Freeman family had their house, we had a built-in tutor and doctor. But we were a healthy lot and did not trouble the physician much. I was the most demanding of the quartet, forever getting tonsillitis. At last it was decided the tonsils must be dealt with. Richard Freeman enlisted the aid of an old colleague, Dr Pitcairn of the Prison Service, and one fateful morning the two arrived with sinister black bags.

I was not only scared, I was starved, not having been allowed to eat any breakfast. However, I found some consolation in the interest shown in me by my brothers, even their ghoulish questions enhanced my sense of importance. When Nanny summoned them for the morning walk, they protested loudly at having to leave me on the steps of the guillotine.

The lookout study was chosen as the operating theatre; for one thing, there was running water next door in my father's dark room. They settled me on a high chair, tilted to an angle, and assured me I would soon be asleep. While he chatted, Dr Pitcairn was dropping a sickly sweet-smelling liquid on to a gauze mask. Where had I smelled that smell before?

'Thank you, Dick, it was very good of you . . .' Cook weeping in the kitchen . . . Miau Puss Cat . . . Struggling with recollection, I drifted away into the land of nowhere as Dr Pitcairn clamped the horrid-smelling mask over my face with a cheerful 'Here we go,' and a voice like mine shouted back, 'No, no!'

5

World events are apt to pass unnoticed by children, unless their own small world is in some way touched or affected by them. I remember the Boer War because, for one thing, my Aunt Lily Hamilton's stepson Harry went off to fight, and before he sailed he came to say goodbye. Harry Hamilton was like one of our lead soldiers come to life, a giant model that we gaped at in admiration. He looked magnificent in scarlet and gold. Strange to think that it was the Boers who taught us the protective value of khaki.

I also remember the day the news came through of the relief of Mafeking City, besieged by the Boers. Constitution Cresent topped one hill and faced another, Windmill Hill, named for the old windmill on its peak. On Mafeking night the flag-waving crowd set fire to the old windmill and made a huge bonfire as well. There were fireworks and singing and a pulsating excitement that lured us all on to the terrace. That was as far as Nanny would let us go in that scene of madness and jubilation.

When we went indoors again Cook produced one of her ginger cakes and glasses of home-made ginger beer. This beer was brewed in a jar kept in the cool stone-flagged passage of the basement. It was Cook's special care. She put in root ginger, well bruised with her rolling pin, added sugar, and filled the jar with water. Then she floated a fungoid blob she called 'me ginger beer plant' on top. This, we understood, was the magic that produced a miracle almost as wonderful as the Bible story of water into wine. The blob grew and spread, like some strange disease, and every odd while Cook slipped off some of its exuberant growths and gave them to her special cronies, so that they could start a home-brew. She mesmerized us into thinking it was the most delicious drink ever made; even better than the sherbet we bought in penny packets.

'Down with them Boers and down with that Mr Kruger,' said

Cook, and we dutifully 'downed' them in her ginger beer. After which, Nanny drove us all upstairs to bed.

Aunt Lily Hamilton was devoted to all of us, and after we left Wimbledon she would have us back to visit, turn and turn about. She had a little Scottie terrier called Jock and half a dozen bantam cocks and hens, kept at the end of the garden. I often wonder why she kept bantams. They do not really make very satisfactory pets, and their minute eggs are no contribution to the breakfast table. But Jock was another matter. Taking Jock for a walk on the Common was as much fun for us as for him. He would rush through the heather and chase rabbits, real or imaginary. At Queen's Mere – the lake enclosed in woodland – he would jump into the water to retrieve the sticks we threw in for him. He was a jolly little dog, except when a muzzle was strapped over his small black nose. These muzzles, made of wire or strips of leather, were sold in every pet shop and came in all shapes and sizes. When the seasonal notice went up in the local police station, they were an obligatory protection against rabies.

My aunt's home, Denmark Cottage, was a neat, little double-fronted house in Denmark Avenue, quite near the Jesuit Church on Edgehill. Part of the pleasure of these visits was being treated as a complete human unit and not as one of a quartet. I helped my aunt around the house. She had no maid, but a daily woman who would turn her hand to cooking, if necessary. Servants, I decided, took a lot of the fun out of life by doing everything for you. My aunt also belonged to several church committees, helping in and organizing bazaars and jumble sales. When a jumble sale was imminent, a big tea chest was carried into the spare room, and as they were donated, all the treasures were carefully stored in it. As a reward for helping to sort them out and wrap them up, I was given a chipped jug with 'A Present from Rye' on one side and a view of the town on the other. I treasured it for years.

A few minutes' walk from Denmark Avenue was a pictur-esque row of cottages, and in one of these lived an old woman known as Granny Green. Granny Green kept and sold ducks. She also baked and sold little cakes, which she declared were concocted from a secret recipe, and were similar to those served for tea at Buckingham Palace. It was really a fearsome thrill whenever Aunt Lily said, 'We'll go and pick up my duck today,' for I had half-deluded myself into believing the old woman was a witch.

Granny had a big Airedale with a bad temper and loud bark. When we rang the bell, Granny, peeping through the curtains, would hastily shut him into the broom cupboard – an indignity which, I am sure, did not improve his temper. Then she opened the door and greetings were exchanged – over a fusillade of barks and thumps. 'All ready for the oven, dear,' she would say, as she preceded us to the kitchen where the duck was laid out for inspection. 'And not a penny extra for doing it for my friends,' she always added, with a sly glance at my aunt. This sales pitch never varied. While Granny wrapped the bird, my aunt would produce her purse. Now, if the current price of ducks was, let us say, six shillings, Granny would say, with a calculating look in her beady little eyes: 'The price went up this week, but I wouldn't dream of charging you more than ten shillings, not a penny more.' And she got away with it. Her victims paid up and returned another day, and the duck and cake industry flourished.

Each of us was given a small garden plot. Mine, though, was the only one to get any real attention. Mustard, cress, and nasturtiums were the nearest my brothers ever got to cultivation. I loved looking at catalogues, and one day my imagination was fired by pictures of a giant marrow. I liked the marrows stuffed with mince which Cook sometimes gave us when they were urged on her by the greengrocer during the summer surplus.

There was a cold frame at the end of the garden, a bit damaged but still recognizable. This, I decided, would be an ideal site for my marrow. But what about the manure I knew was essential for its growth? Frankie Mason, paying us one of his visits, solved the problem.

'The mailcart,' he said tersely. 'It's kept in the basement, isn't it?' I nodded. 'Well, we'll wheel it out, put an old box on the front seat, and get the shovel out of the cellar. Easy,' he finished, with a confidence I did not share.

It was far from easy. The housemaid was no problem, for she was busy polishing silver in her pantry, but we had to wait until Cook was having her afternoon nap and Nanny was busy in the nursery. At last we succeeded in getting the mailcart out, silently closing the back door after us.

That was the day of the horse, and once we were clear of Constitution Crescent, there was plenty of manure. Frankie took hold of the shafts and pulled the mailcart, while I shovelled up the precious stuff. Then, to my horror, I saw Colonel Arathoon approaching. A birthday party was coming up at Parrock Manor where the Arathoons lived, and I did not want this treat to be jeopardized. I panicked, opened a gate, and darted into a strange front garden. Better to be shouted at by an angry householder than to miss a party; and who would invite a child who scraped up manure from the road? I breathed a quiet prayer of thanks when, after a few minutes, I dared peep through the hedge, and saw Colonel Arathoon's back retreating down the road.

'What on earth?' exclaimed Frankie.

'Hush,' I cautioned, 'someone else might be coming.'

Cook opened the door to us, and a look of scandalized disbelief came over her face. She and Nanny were about to confiscate the precious manure, when Richard Austin Freeman and my mother came to the rescue. I heard the word 'initiative' and that seemed to turn the balance in our favour. But, like Herbert Spencer, the philosopher he admired, Richard Freeman believed the punishment should fit the crime. Frankie and I were given a scrubbing brush each and a bucket of soapy water and told to clean the desecrated mailcart.

There were no houses opposite our half-finished crescent. A rusty railing snaked down the hill and enclosed a totally neglected garden. Right at the foot of the hill, hidden from the road, was a house. Here lived an old eccentric, whose name I have forgotten. Dickens was my favourite author on the occasion of my one and only visit to the hidden house, so I called the man Fagin.

We envied him one thing – an extraordinary 'Folly' he had built of lumps of slag from coal waste, called 'klinkers'. The Folly was a square pillar on four struts, topped by a concrete platform. It commanded a wonderful view of the river, and the trees and bushes of the garden spread like a sea of green leaves beneath it. To reach the platform, an iron ladder had been embedded in the klinker casing.

One day my father announced that he had to see our neighbour on business. Cuthbert and I looked at each other. 'Take us with you,' we begged. And to our delight, he did. Down the hill we trotted beside him. At the foot of the hill we pushed open a tall wrought-iron gate with creaking hinges. The house was dark and forbidding, with ivy that half-covered some of the windows. In front of the door was a mat which said 'Beware of the Dog'. But there was no barking when my father pulled the bell and we could hear the jangling summons. Before the clamour ceased, the door was opened and there stood Fagin, smiling a senile welcome.

'The dog won't bite you, my little dears,' he said, pointing to the inside mat, which read, 'WARE Be the Dog?'. This we considered the funniest joke we had ever heard, even funnier than the comics we bought with our pocket money of sixpence a week, but we were too scared to laugh at the time. Then an idea flashed into my mind. 'May we wait outside?' I whispered to my father. Old Fagin beamed his approval. 'Yes, you do that, my little dears,' he said, as he ushered Father into the dark hall crowded with all kinds of junk.

Dismissed by a nod from Father, I lost not a moment. 'Come on quick,' I told Cuthbert, who was always ready to follow my lead. We ran up the twisting overgrown path, undeterred by nettle or bramble, till we reached the Folly, climbed the ladder, and stood on the small platform with all the world, it seemed, spread out before us. 'Oh, if we could only picnic here,' I sighed. A picnic was the seal of ultimate approval. I pulled two pieces of toffee out of my pocket and handed one to Cuthbert – 'Let's pretend.'

Another eccentric in our lives was Cook's sister, a widow who lived in a derelict house within an easy walk of the Crescent. 'Sister' was described as having 'legs that double under her, Ma'am'. She was looked after by a neighbour, and Cook spent every spare moment 'doing' for this sister, who was an autocrat in a Bath chair.

In those says, there were two kinds of Bath chair. One was a light wickerwork three-wheeled carriage with a steering bar fixed to the small front wheel. The bar turned left or right at the twist of a wrist. Those who had chronic invalids or old people to look after nearly always possessed one of these. The other type, found in all seaside and spa resorts (like the Bath it was named for), was a ponderous affair, with a hood one could raise or lower and an oilcloth apron to protect knees from rain. A professional attendant pushed these bulky affairs along the promenade, charging so much an hour for hire of himself and his chair.

Cook's sister had one of the wickerwork sort – a bit worse for the wear, like herself. One seldom saw her out of it. On occasion, the neighbour would wheel her up to our house for a cup of tea with Cook. Her birthday, a well-advertised event, was one such occasion, and Cook had made a large currant cake with icing. Our mother gave us presents to wrap, and after our own tea we trooped down to the kitchen. There we found the three women: the neighbour who 'looked after'; Cook in her best white cap and apron; and 'Sister' in her best bonnet, a marvellous affair of black, slightly rusty velvet, decorated by bows and sequins and beads, and tied under her chin by a bow of black ribbon. She sat in her chair, her bony knees covered with a plaid shawl, another shawl over her shoulders. She was made entirely of skin and bone. The yellowing skin of her face was tight over the cheek bones; the scant hair was drawn back from the shiny forehead. Her eyes were glassy, like those of a dead fish. Cook once confided to my mother that Sister had 'fits'. 'Applelepsy, Ma'am,' she said. Tied to the leg of the kitchen table was the tethered cat she was never without.

We mumbled our 'Happy Birthdays' as instructed, and laid our present on the plaid rug. Cake was distributed all round. In the now relaxed atmosphere, Cuthbert, who was a devil for facts, asked Sister how old she was. 'Well, not to be telling you lies, young gentleman, I'm as old as my tongue and a little older than my teeth.'

But Cuthbert had heard that one before. 'Are you a hundred?' he asked. 'Well, I'm not the sister of Methusaleh, Master Cuthbert. And you just tell me how old the Good Book says Methusaleh was?' and her skinny finger stabbed at his bewildered face.

I can well believe, when I look back through the years into those glassy eyes, that Sister was an epileptic; however, she was also an opportunist. Was she really as infirm as she made herself out to be? Nanny had just returned from taking a bundle of garments to the lady, she and my mother having had one of their 'turnouts' of clothes closets, and I remember hearing her say to my mother, 'And there she was, in the back yard, on her two legs, hanging out the clothes. Spry as you like – till she saw me.'

In my childhood there were no large stores selling inexpensive clothes for children, clothes not made to survive, not worth alteration or repair. Our clothes were made to last, and hence 'The Little Woman'. A lady with money or title had her own personal maid, who combined hairdressing, valeting, and subsidiary dressmaking. But the middle-class housewife had to be content with her 'little woman'. There were two types. One was the dressmaker who lived in a small house in a side street. You took bales of silk or cloth to her. After consultation and a conning of the tattered fashion books on the table in her front room, you retired to her back premises and removed your top layer for her to take your measurements. To find her, you looked in all the lace-curtained front windows until, yes, there it was, the big placard hanging between the curtains: 'Miss So-and-So, Court Dressmaker'. What did this mean? Court Dressmaker? Not even Nanny could answer that one. They all seemed to be spinsters, and that was another puzzling thing about them.

The other type of 'little woman' came to your house on a once-a-week basis or when summoned. A room was set aside for her on that day. You put a sewing machine under a window to get a good light and provided pins and other accessories. That 'little woman' really earned her money – household linen to be repaired; sheets sides-to-middle; skirts to be shortened or lengthened; new linings to coats; new collars to shirts – there was nothing she could not deal with.

Most of these women seemed to suffer from some form of indigestion, and who could wonder. Our Miss Saunders, putting up an apologetic hand, complained genteelly of 'the wind'. She was always given a luncheon tray. 'Such a lovely dinner your mother gives me,' she remarked one day. 'Not like some. The richer the meaner, if you ask me. A nice bit of cheese for the mice, and the parings for me,' she added darkly. 'Who gave you parings?' I asked with much interest. 'Ah, that would be telling, wouldn't it,' she replied, brightly discreet. And the flow of gossip went on, unnamed clients and their affairs an outlet for her own restricted life with its iron boundaries of work and poverty.

51

Clothes were washed with Sunlight soap, which came in bars. It was Cook's job to take her sharpest knife and cut these bars into sizeable pieces and put them to dry out on a shelf in her pantry. For cleaning things like baths and sinks, we used Monkey soap – so called because the wrapper showed a monkey as its trademark. It was a gritty soap, with more powdered pumice than fat in it. For personal use, there was Pear's soap for the grown-ups, clear and beautiful to look at, like jelly. For us, there was Wright's coal tar soap to cope with our dirt and abrasions.

As for cosmetics, few people used them. A dab of powder on a shiny nose was enough for most women. Frankie's mother, Lily Mason, used a very simple form of make-up. We would watch, fascinated, as she sat in front of the dressing table mirror in our spare room and dabbed rouge on her cheeks, spreading it with a hare's foot. After which, she took the lid off her ivory powder box and dusted powder over the rouge with a fluffy powder puff. She was a beautiful woman, and when this exercise was completed, we thought she looked like a fairy queen.

Our own mother used no make-up at all.

Sunday was the day for going to Mass and coming home to a breakfast of bacon and eggs and fat brown sausages. No work was supposed to be done that was not strictly necessary. Not even needlework. No novels to be read before lunch (but this rule applied to weekdays as well).

Sunday luncheon was almost a ritual. Grace was said by my father, standing at the head of the table. A sirloin of roast beef was carried in under a shining metal cover, which reflected and distorted our faces into those of expectant goblins. Yorkshire pudding and baked potatoes; then fruit pie and custard or cream; cheese and biscuits to top up. We lived well in those days. This meal was generally followed by a family walkabout along the country lanes that wound their peaceful way to Singlewell, Cobham and Wrotham. We were not enthusiastic about these walks; for one thing, we had to wear our best clothes, and tempting puddles or beckoning berries nodding to us from the hedges had to be passed by. No doubt, however, these walks helped digest the roast beef or boiled mutton with caper sauce of our standard Sunday luncheon.

Walks with Nanny were quite different. The hedgerows were our treasure house, with flowers and fruit for us to gather, frogs, toads and lizards to dislodge from underneath their sheltering roots and leaves.

On a few rare occasions Richard Freeman and our mother took 'the class' out for a nature study. This was quite exciting because it seemed to us that he knew about the lifestyle of everything that crept or crawled or flew. His magnetic eyes seemed to draw them out of holes and crevasses for our benefit and instruction. A freshly deceased bird or mole was picked up and taken home for dissection. I well recall these demonstrations.

Richard, pipe in mouth, carpet slippers on feet, would bend over the small corpse, the shining scalpel poised for the first incision, whilst we, the audience, watched with breathless interest. A quick cut and the tiny organ was held up for inspection. 'What is this? What is its function?' When our pet hedgehog, Algy, fell down the area steps and died, he found his way to the dissecting table, and later to a kind of practical immortality, when I made his shell into a pincushion by pressing a red velvet ball stuffed with bran into his middle. My brothers were very envious of this treasure.

Out walking, one happened on more than one quaint oast house with its bent chimney, where hops were dried. Once a year, before the summer sun had left us, Gravesend was invaded by an industrial army from the East End of London: the hop pickers. Special trains were laid on for them. I remember seeing them, men, women, and children, trudging along the Wrotham road on their way to the gardens where the hops swung on long trails of green, leafy vines that hung from pole to pole. This area of Kent was famous for its hops.

Nanny was a Kentish girl, who never wholly lost the Kentish burr in her speech. She would take us to the nearest hop garden to help with the picking. Whole families sat or stood around the baskets, picking the pale green tassels from the vines twisted round the poles, now laid in rows on the ground to be stripped of their harvest. Nanny would choose what she considered the most respectable looking family and offer our services. These were gratefully accepted, for payment was by the bushel, and every extra pair of hands was valuable.

The aromatic smell of the hops was penetrating, and the

warm sunshine and our crushing fingers brought out its potency. This practical lesson in the pleasure and satisfaction to be gained by lending a helping hand is a lesson framed in the beauty of pale green tassels on dark green leaves and, overhead, a blue sky and drifting white clouds.

Did we say our prayers? Yes, we did. We asked for all the possible and impossible things that children ask for. Our faith was kept alive because the possible was answered by the loving eavesdropping of Nanny or our parents.

6

The Catholic Church in Gravesend was an ugly but spacious building in the middle of town. There were two leading Catholic families – the Arnolds and the Chadwicks. Old Mr Arnold was brother to Sir Edwin Arnold, whose book *The Light of Asia* won him recognition in his time. The Mr Arnold we knew was head of the firm of solicitors Arnold, Chadwick and Chadwick, and a real patriarch. Most of the Chadwick women of the second generation were née Arnold. In the third generation, there was a preponderance of girls, all dutiful daughters and pious Catholics. They were very much cast in the same mould – long pale faces and long thin bodies – and so many were the ramifications of the Arnold-Chadwick clan, that the dutiful daughters were never out of mourning. Occasionally they escaped as far as 'half-mourning' of mauve or grey, but, before they could plunge into the motley of colour, another death would appear in the columns of *The Times* and back they would be in black.

We rented a pew not far behind them. Our father paid so much a quarter and slipped his visiting card into one of the little brass frames found in all the front pews. Woe betide the outsider who tried to gatecrash a rented pew. There were a few free seats in the back of the building. There were also Board Schools and workhouses for the poorer brethren. But at least the Catholic Church admitted the poor and the derelict, even if they did have to sit hidden and forgotten at the back of the temple. The Church of England belonged wholly to the middle class. God was their God – exclusively. They put on top hat and frock coat and went to church on Sunday to thank Him for their blessings. The artistocracy were gods unto themselves, and the working class had little for which to thank anyone. Yet they kept alive their faith in chapels across the country – dim grey buildings in the back streets of big cities.

The Catholic Church stood aloof and unbending, but a

spiritual force to be reckoned with – loved by those within her walls, hated by her enemies without.

A little later than most Catholic children, I made my first Communion when I was eleven. Miss Saunders was called in to make the dress. I followed her into the room set aside for the occasion and listened with suppressed excitement whilst she and my mother went into conference with pattern books and a roll of white silk.

'Being Chapel myself,' Miss Saunders told Nanny when Nanny brought her a cup of tea, 'I don't hold with all this dressing up.' She stood back, her head cocked, to see the result after pinning a sleeve in place. Nanny allowed herself a genteel sniff of disapproval as she set the cup down on the table. Nanny was High Church (Catholicism without the Pope) and more tolerant of him than she was of chapel-goers. She was really a snob at heart. Classless herself, by reason of her rejection of the class into which she had been born, she was passionately protective of the gentry and what was expected of them.

All that day Miss Saunders snipped and measured and disapproved, and the result was a dress that did her credit. It was white silk with a tightly fitting bodice, tucked and boned. Lace epaulettes lent width to my narrow shoulders, and the skirt, ending in a lace flounce, was a grown-up ankle length. Round my waist was a wide sash, which Miss Saunders tied in a bow at the back. She then retreated a pace or two to view the whole effect. 'And very nice, too,' she remarked, 'though I says it as shouldn't.'

A week later I knelt at the altar, one of five or six white-clad figures. I felt that something wonderful was about to happen. And it did. Through almost ninety years I've clung to my faith. From the archaic teaching of the penny catechism; through the controversy over 'the pill'; through, and in spite of, hundreds of boring sermons.

The penny catechism was learned by rote, question and answer. I was always fascinated by the chapter on sin. First, it was divided into two categories, mortal and venial. That, for a start, was alarming to a child's mind. Where, exactly, did venial sin end and mortal sin take over? Amongst the sins listed were some rather obscure ones called 'sins against the Holy Ghost'. Then there were 'sins crying to heaven for vengeance'. One of these was 'defrauding labourers of their wages'. And of course, there were the 'seven deadly sins'. Gluttony was included in this last category, which rather troubled me. Could three helpings of bird's nest pudding be classified as gluttony?

Going to Confession was a scary thing in itself. The dark box, the grille through which one saw the listening profile of the priest – one's mind became a blank, and one's tongue tied. The kindly priest would come to the rescue by suggesting all sorts of unlikely temptations. But the real trouble was finding enough sins to make the recounting worthwhile. I found myself blowing up an incident such as sneaking chocolate to make it sound like a bank robbery.

Then there was the rule about fasting from midnight before Communion. Cleaning one's teeth in the morning was a real hazard, for one might inadvertently swallow a few drops of water, and I was a child who was apt to get scruples about such things. Nanny was a great help here. 'Why nonsense,' she would say, 'even the Pope himself must swallow a few drops of water when he cleans his teeth, and he's not put out.' She spoke with a conviction that carried total reassurance.

My father had two sisters who were nuns. The younger we rarely saw. Aunt Gertie, the elder, was a teacher of English in the Holy Child order and a sporadic but lasting influence on my life. From our Aunt Florence she had heard the very worst interpretation put upon my mother's friendship with Richard Austin Freeman. She also considered that the irregular and undisciplined type of education I was getting could hardly produce a first-class citizen.

One day in midsummer she appeared in person to state her case. We were waiting on the terrace when the station fly deposited the two black-robed figures on our doorstep. As Aunt Gertie stooped to peck at our cheeks we were conscious of the stiff white linen coif that framed her face. It was very difficult to kiss a nun dressed in the habit of those days. No nun travelled alone then, so Nanny took charge of the little lay sister who accompanied our aunt, giving our mother and her visitor the privacy they needed.

Told to wait for an hour or so, the cabby got down from his perch and, removing the bit from the horse's mouth, produced a nose-bag. We stood around and watched while he put it over the animal's head. He must have been an unusually kind man, we thought, for it was a very hot day and the horse's ears stuck through a little straw hat. It was not unusual to see big draught horses, sweating under their loads, drawing ploughs over sun-baked fields, wearing these ridiculous straw hats, but the ordinary cabby seldom treated his horse to one.

'Does he like wearing a hat?' I ventured.

The man's weather-beaten face crinkled into a smile. 'He likes it better'n I do,' he said, removing a battered bowler from his head. He wiped his glistening scalp with his bandanna. The working man did not wear a collar and tie – he knotted a voluminous square of red cotton round his neck. A bandanna was also used to cover the pudding basin containing his dinner, which was brought to him by his wife or child if he was working anywhere near home.

As our friend replaced his hat, Cook appeared with an invitation to come in for a bite and a drink. This was gratefully accepted. He led his horse across the road and hitched it to the railings of old Fagin's estate. 'He won't run away, not with that nosebag on,' he assured us. 'You youngsters watch him for me.' This we agreed to do. But there was nothing to watch, so now that the grown-ups were safely indoors, we found a piece of chalk and marked out a hopscotch pitch on the pavement. Hopscotch on a public footpath was definitely not a thing that Nanny would approve. But it certainly was a hot day, and this was an opportunity not to be lost.

Meanwhile, poor Aunt Gertie was waging battle on my behalf. But she was defeated even before she had started. My parents were far too committed to the status quo and to Richard Austin Freeman even to consider change.

When does childhood end? For me, perhaps, with my first period. But I am not sure. We called it 'the curse' in those days, a sort of code word for women. I was told what would happen and how to cope, but the significance was left unexplained. 'It's to do with having babies' was as far as Nanny would go. There were taboos attached. At these times one must not ride a bicycle or go for a swim. And on no account must the men in one's life even guess at the reason for the refusal. A headache was a socially acceptable excuse, like the 'not at home' if one didn't want visitors. Spades were never called spades where sex was concerned. The word pregnant was not used except by the medical profession. Sex and the mechanics of sex were concealed behind a façade of sham innocence and ignorance: adult evasion of a duty to reveal the facts of life and love.

Or perhaps my childhood really ended with that passionate kiss on the Sussex Downs? A kiss that finally destroyed the protective chrysalis of innocence. I was staying with the Mason family at Ditchling, where they lived the 'simple life' of luxury. Ditchling was a show village in Sussex, and Farm Corner was a glorified cottage. The garden was a masterpiece of landscaping.

They had a cook, whom Lily Mason's friends were always trying to bribe away from her, and a young housemaid, Julia, a country girl little older than I. How happy I felt as I opened my suitcase in the charming chintzy bedroom that was to be mine for a whole week. I looked forward to the tray Julia would bring me in the morning. Early morning tea, with two wafers of bread and butter – this was the good life, like a sandwich with the crusts trimmed off. Yet, as I looked out of the casement window at the sunlit garden with the rose beds and flower borders, I felt that I was missing something. I was, in fact, falling in love with love. In my day, this meant turning to Rossetti, Tennyson and Browning.

Frankie arrived on the second day of my visit, throwing his cap in the air. School days were over. Cambridge and independence waited for him in the autumn. We hadn't much to say to each other that first day. We were meeting on unfamiliar ground, two young adults in an adult world, almost like strangers. The next day he said, out of the blue, 'Let's take bikes and explore.' I hesitated for a moment. It was a lovely day, with warm sunshine drying the little pearls of dew upon the lawn. Well, why not? So I borrowed Julia's bike and off we went.

'You've changed a lot,' he said, as we pedalled along side by side. 'You're quite a good-looker – or didn't you know?'

I nodded. 'I know. You're not the first one who's told me so.' Then I added, 'So have you.'

'So have I what?' His bike nearly wobbled into mine.

'Changed, silly.' The preliminary inanities had now been exchanged. There was a coppice we were passing.

'Let's leave our bikes here,' he said. 'There's shade under those trees up on the hill.' So we jumped off and laid our bikes under some bushes. Then we sat on a carpet of warm brown leaves under the beech trees. Not near each other. Feet apart. No, inches. Closer. Touching. And then it came – the inevitable moment – crushing arms, lips pressed to mine. The primitive that drew yet repelled. I might have been skinny, but I was wiry. I broke loose.

'You beast,' I said, which was what, I feel sure, I was supposed to say. And I ran towards the bikes.

That night, for the first time ever, I locked my door. I lay awake in the darkness, and childhood was a thing of the past. Shocked, yet thrilled, I was conscious of a secret power. And behind my locked door I slept. In the morning I found a note slipped under the door. It read: *I was a cad. I'm going to stay with the aunts in Brighton. Forgive me. Frank.*

And so we leave the child that was:

> *Standing with reluctant feet,*
> *Where the brook and river meet,*
> *Womanhood and childhood fleet.*

Part Two

The Years Between

7

The years between my cushioned childhood and the First World War were years of rather aimless frustration. They were also years of making do and doing without, when comfort and security suddenly became words without meaning. Grand-father, source and provider of both these things, was 'ham-mered' on the London Stock Exchange. Disgraced and declared bankrupt, he died not long afterwards, a broken man, leaving a legacy of debt and poverty to my parents.

I remember the day of his funeral because it seemed to emphasize the gloom that hung over our future, blacker than the pall on his coffin. There was none of the attendant pomp of a funeral of that time, for such things cost money. A black hearse drawn by two black horses was followed by one carriage, into which were packed my parents, the officiating priest, and myself. I think my mother never forgave Aunt Florence her heartless rejection of her own father. She was not even a mourner at his funeral.

Grandfather was buried in that portion of Gravesend cemetery set aside for the Catholic dead. In the years of his prosperity he had built for himself a hideous grey stone mausoleum, like a Stone Age treasure chest. As we stood around this macabre symbol of family unity, I noted the blank plaques where, presumably, the names of my own parents would be inscribed, and I wept for them in a sort of fantastic realization of an end whose beginning was only a promise.

'I am the Resurrection and the Life,' intoned the red-faced Irish priest, before pausing to blow his nose on a rather grimy handkerchief. The ugly and the sordid, the sublime and the absurd were there at the burying of a man who had lived without love. My mother's eyes were wet with tears as we left him there, waiting for his family to join him, and returned to the mean little house that was now our home.

It was a shabby, semi-detached house in Clarence Place, at

the foot of Windmill Hill, with a basement and discoloured stone steps leading up to a front door that had needed a coat of paint for many years. When the front door was opened, one walked into a narrow little hall with brown linoleum underfoot and dark brown varnished walls rubbed to unsightly patches here and there. A door to a small garden faced you, and behind this door was a loo with a chain that seemed to unleash the waters of Niagara. This was a source of social embarrassment, which kept one imprisoned if the doorbell rang at the same time. There were two small rooms on every floor; it was like a home-made doll's house put together in a hurry. Gone was the graciousness of living, the space and luxury of Constitution Crescent – we were like boxed-up mice, I sometimes thought. And yet as a family we did not suffer. Looking back I realize this was a great achievement on the part of our parents. We felt neither resentment nor frustration.

Cuthbert, I think, was hit the hardest. Long afterwards he told me how he hated that mean little house and had schemed and struggled to get away from it. I was not of an enquiring turn of mind where practical matters were concerned. I never wondered where the money came from for our daily bread. Like Elijah, I felt that the Lord would provide, though not of course in the guise of ministering ravens. I was not the least worried; Nanny was with us. She was now cook, housemaid, and, as always, the cornerstone of our security.

In due course my father was taken on by another firm of stockbrokers. The Freeman family no longer needed his backing; Richard was now doing quite well, and a 'For Sale' board swung on the railing of Number 2 Woodville Terrace. My education, such as it was, now faded into a sporadic reading of unrelated subjects in books borrowed from the Free Library. My brothers went to classes at the local Technical School, their total ignorance of mathematics remedied by coaching from a bird-like woman who seemed undaunted by their abysmal lack of knowledge.

Why I was not considered worthy of further instruction I shall never know. Perhaps finances would not stretch even to classes at the Technical School. The comfortable theory that learning was not so important for a girl would have been forgivable if marriage, the recognized vocation of every girl, had seemed a likely possibility. But how could the necessary ground bait of even mild entertaining possibly attract eligibles to the genteel poverty of Number 38 Clarence Place?

The loss of a comfortable living was the final circumstance among many that had set me peculiarly adrift as far as any social life was concerned. I had missed the automatic training in social intercourse that school would have brought. And my mother had shown a somewhat benign indifference to society, making little effort to introduce me to its ways. So I poured out my adolescent romantic dreams in poems and rode about the lovely Kentish lanes on my bicycle. Sometimes I sat by the wayside with sketching block and box of watercolours someone had given me – a lonely girl of sixteen, unaware that it was loneliness she was feeling.

When I was seventeen my last link with childhood memories of Wimbledon was suddenly torn away. Aunt Lily, whom I loved, was now a widow and was dying of cancer. In those days no-one spoke openly of cancer, but we all knew that she was suffering from it. She asked for me, and one black day her stepson Harry came to fetch me to Denmark Cottage.

That journey to Wimbledon seemed to go on for ever. I stared out of the carriage window, seeing the fields and the straggling houses slipping by in a mist of tears, only dimly aware of the sprawl of outer London as we neared Charing Cross. Out of one train and into another, past the sooty rows of mean little houses like our home in Clarence Place, my thoughts urged the engine onwards, as it puffed and whistled its way through the darkening landscape.

The lamps were lit on Wimbledon station and along the familiar streets. 'Don't be afraid,' my cousin whispered, as he pushed open the garden gate of Denmark Cottage. But I was afraid. That front door had opened up to so many happy hours, but now what should I find beyond it? I followed Harry up the stairs, and there, on the small square landing, was Mabel, another cousin, who had trained as a nurse. As she took my hand to lead me into the sick room she whispered, 'She is sleeping now. Come in and sit beside her bed so that you will be the first thing she sees when she wakes up.'

Aunt Lily looked so little changed as she lay there in the big brass bed that a quiver of hope flickered up – and then died. No, this was different. Shaded lamplight showed the sharp lines that pain had drawn. The loved face was pale and shrunken when I looked more closely. They had operated weeks before, but the slow malignant cancer had returned. Mabel never let me see Aunt Lily suffer, but in the short intervals between the spells of pain I sat beside her and held her hand.

'Don't cry, darling,' she would whisper. 'It means so much to have you here.' So I stayed on, and when I went to bed at night little creeping fears crawled into bed with me, and the sense of loss was like a weight pressing down on me. In the daytime I escaped into trivial acts or sat, holding the hand that was light as a withered leaf in mine. Sometimes I read her poetry or bits out of the New Testament.

Then one day Mabel came to the room where I was dressing to go out. 'She looks bad,' she said, 'and her pulse is very weak. Will you run up to the presbytery – she should have the last sacraments.' She put an arm round my shoulder as she spoke. 'Don't cry, child. These last two days the pain has been getting beyond drugs, and the sacrament will bring comfort to her.' So I raced up the hill to the great Jesuit church, rock-like against a grey winter sky. Sobbing and breathless, I knocked on the presbytery door.

Late that afternoon my parents arrived, summoned by Mabel. As I tiptoed out of the room for the last time, I knew that peace and death were not far off now. My father took me home, but my mother stayed to the end. Long afterwards, I learned that Lily Hamilton had left the bulk of her money to me. She was not well off, but this legacy explained why, in the years to come, I was able to visit Italy and Brittany, and why I never really felt deprived, as I am sure my parents felt deprived, in those later years.

But why was I never told of this money? Why was I not allowed to be responsible for the management of some of it? We were not encouraged to ask such questions, and I for my part was totally lacking in curiosity as to the whys and wherefores of the realistic and practical aspects of life. My friends lived between the pages of books. No-one asked me, 'What are you going to do with your life?' Indeed, it was characters like me who were clogging the wheels of the Pankhurst machine.

Social happenings in my life were rare and literally written in red ink in my diary. The odd subscription dance in a dreary room in the Clarendon Hotel by the river had all the glamour of a Cinderella ball. My mother's friend Gertrude Pinching was my sponsor and chaperone. Such affairs were outside the scope of my mother's curtailed social activities. She had her few friends and enjoyed them, but she felt out of the picture when confronted with large-scale social activities. Possibly she thought of herself as a reject, and almost certainly the buying of an evening dress was out of the question.

Gertrude Pinching and her friends on the Hospital Committee ran teas for the benefit of the hospital, whose finances always seemed in need of a boost. Once a year there was a fête in Rocherville Gardens, a fast decaying replica of the once famous Vauxhall Gardens. The gardens were gay with sideshows, overgrown shrubberies decked out with lanterns that were lighted when the evening shadows descended and turned the whole scene into a fairyland. I was proud to tie a muslin apron round my waist and help out as a waitress, dashing about with pots of tea and plates of cakes in the tea enclosure.

Then, also on behalf of the hospital, posters were put out (gaudy, hand-made affairs) to advertise the fact that such-and-such a play was to be performed by the Gravesend Amateur Dramatic Society. I was swept into the Dramatic Society with a walk-on part in *As You Like It*. But, although I enjoyed the fun of rehearsals, I felt no yearning for the stage. Furthermore, Shakespeare bored me, and Shakespearian plays were usually the ones chosen.

Aunt Florence, now married at the age of fifty to a surgeon in the Navy, made occasional half-hearted attempts to launch me on society. When they were stationed at Sheerness, she asked me there for a visit, as there was to be what she grandly called a Naval ball. As soon as I arrived, Timmins was called in to run me up a white satin dress, and I have no doubt that as far as looks went I did my aunt and uncle credit. But what everyone seemed to forget was that nobody had taught me to dance. And to add to the fiasco of that night, my aunt made me carry a bouquet of flowers. There I stood, clutching the unwanted bunch of flowers with one hand and a programme with a dangling pencil in the other, and wishing that the beeswax-polished floor would open up and swallow me.

The evening was saved by an elderly captain putting his name down for the supper dances on my shamefully blank programme. Here I was on safer ground, for I enjoyed good food and, given a sympathetic listener, I could talk. The fact that he sent me a box of chocolates the next day was, I suspect, due more to his sympathy than to my charm.

Other relatives all made sporadic attempts to brighten life for a penniless girl who was something of an oddity, with no idea of how to dress, or dance, or flirt – shortcomings that cancelled out the appeal of a pretty face. Even old Aunt Gussie (my great-aunt, really) had me to stay in her neat little villa on the seafront at Weymouth. Here she lived with a meek and downtrodden companion, who not only fetched and carried for Aunt Gussie, but who was also the slave of a waddling pug dog with bulging eyes.

Poor Miss Booth! She made delicious home-baked bread and dainty invalid dishes, but like many women with neither husband nor special skills, she would end up as a 'decayed gentlewoman', lucky if some charitable institution took her up as a 'case'. From this eye-opening visit, I made up my mind that never ever would I become an old lady's companion. This was not a constructive state of mind, but it proved to be protective.

Having lost the battle to get me into good Catholic society as a pupil at the convent at St Leonard's, Aunt Gertie was keeping a watchful eye on me, for I certainly seemed in need of a guardian angel or a guiding hand. She arrived one day, a lovely day in June, and we settled her in the least hazardous of our three garden chairs. 'Dorothy, dear,' she began, 'what are you thinking of doing? At eighteen I expect you have some ideas.'

I was sitting on the grass at her feet, and I looked up at the kind little monkey face, surrounded by its glazed white linen frame. 'I don't know,' I said. 'I wish I did.'

She took a letter from a capacious pocket. 'Here,' she said, 'is a proposition which may help you.' She put on a pair of steel-rimmed glasses and proceeded to read the letter. It was from a Mrs So-and-So, a hyphened name I have now forgotten, who was looking for a girl from a good Catholic family to be her companion. She then listed the requirements for this paragon.

I shook my head. 'Aunt Gertie,' I said, 'what she wants is a slave. And I'd rather be penniless and free and stuck here.

Anyway, I'd be nearly penniless with what she calls "pin money".'

'Don't be hasty,' she admonished, 'this woman is a good Catholic, goes to Mass every day, and she is planning a pilgrimage to Lourdes this summer. And you could go with her. Think of that!'

Poor Aunt Gertie. Not even the prospect of Lourdes could change my mind. Sadly, she replaced the letter, and as she did so, she quickly withdrew her hand from the generous pocket. 'The cork has come out!' was her horrified and cryptic remark. 'Reverend Mother would insist on my bringing it in case of emergency.' The strong smell of brandy was self-explanatory.

We did the best we could for her. Nanny brought out a bowl of soapy water and a sponge, but I have a suspicion that a few faint whiffs lingered on to bring scandal into the second-class compartment in which she travelled back to London.

When I was about nineteen, Frankie Mason's parents suggested I went with them to a villa in Italy which was their retreat from the boredom of an English winter. So one day in mid-September, limp after a rough Channel crossing, I found myself packed into a carriage with voluble French and Italian travellers, chugging along through a country whose roads and rivers all seemed to be lined with poplar trees. My first experience of the sights, sounds, and smells of the Continent was intoxicating. When we were swallowed up into the dark mouth of the Simplon tunnel, I sat back and, deprived of the landscape, took stock of my fellow travellers.

My host and hostess were not with me in the economy-class compartment, but paid visits at intervals. That carriageful of people was certainly a broadening influence on my still Victorian outlook on life. The fat woman nursing her baby openly and unashamed, the polite, black-whiskered gentleman bowing me into the primitive lavatory compartment – both swept aside the smug conventions by which I had been brought up. And when we came out at the other end of the tunnel, I gazed, fascinated, on to the Swiss valleys and their grazing cows and doll's house chalets.

We spent the night at a hotel in Milan before going on to Florence. A brief visit to the cathedral there made little impact on me – I had seen other beautiful cathedrals – but the reeking, noisy railway carriage and the woman nursing her baby and tucking her breasts into her unbuttoned blouse are still vivid memories.

Florence – the then-unspoiled city lying in the valley of the Arno. Florence, with its bridges and its built-to-last-for-ever palaces; its street latrines with gay advertisements where men walked in in the middle of a conversation and out again, as casual as you please, to continue that conversation. Florence shook me out of my personal unsatisfactory present and enveloped me in the beauty of an eternal Renaissance.

That visit to Italy was not really a practical solution for the loneliness of my adolescence. It provided me with a scrapbook for lovely pictures, but not with a guide book to channel awakening emotions into productivity. I drifted along, wandering amongst the olive groves of Fiesole, where the pale pink cyclamens grew amongst the grey shale boulders. I was transiently happy. Each day brought its own novel enjoyment. Breakfast was on the gravelled terrace beneath a line of rusting holm oaks; little sweet black grapes and green figs, their crimson flesh warm from the sunshine of a new day, were eaten with the slightly sour white bread freshly baked by Domenico, the cook.

There were luncheon parties and tea parties. The English colony in Florence built its life on the pleasant trivia of self-imposed exile. There was the elderly couple, Pompey and Daisy, who had become an institution. There were the singers: Emerson, a tall, dark young man who was not so young, and Blue Boy, a fair-haired and blue-eyed light tenor who seemed to have no other name. I was too unsophisticated to guess at the relationship that the English colony accepted with whispering condonation. I doubt that the word 'homosexual' had even come into my vocabulary.

And there was Miss Burke, whose tea parties had the atmosphere of a salon. She was a regal and, it seemed to me, a very old lady. And she had a very, very old dog, whose habits were certainly not suited to the gay and chic people who talked and laughed and drank orange pekoe out of fragile china cups. I usually sat silent at her tea parties. As a rule there was no-one of my own generation with whom I could communicate. This tight little circle shared its interests and its gossip and the repartee that was fashionable at that time, so that I felt shut out. This was a cluster of people who played at being happy and cultured.

But one afternoon a young Italian entered the magic circle and was obviously lost in the barrage of intimate conversation. A common isolation drew us together. For once I talked and laughed and even tried to rise to a mild flirtation. And then it happened – the slow, insidious smell there was no mistaking. My cheeks flamed. Surely, surely, he would not think I could be guilty of such a revolting breach of good manners? The culprit, lying beside my chair, made no move. I felt suspended in a real and mental miasma. 'Signorina,' said the quiet voice of my companion, 'let us move to other chairs – the smell of the old dog is not so good.' It was as simple as that. My Victorian 'niceness' and prudishness melted away. I had learned a lesson.

Lily Mason was a leader in this tight little community. Beautiful and always beautifully dressed, she also had a witty tongue. I felt like a dull little nobody on the edge of the circle that surrounded her. She always had one obvious male slave in attendance, to pull out a chair, hold her parasol, and generally fetch and carry.

One of these slaves was a German we spoke of as 'the Baron'. He was a portly man who wore an eyeglass on a ribbon. He owned a bulldog who wore a fantastic collar made like a fur ruff. It was very often my fate to chaperone expeditions to galleries and shops when they went into Florence for the day. Lily Mason and her cavalier walked on ahead, whilst I held the bulldog's leash. He had a nice taste in lampposts. 'Now she will have to wait,' the Baron would remark, looking round and twirling his moustache complacently. I think he resented me as a chaperone. Sometimes I resented it myself.

I would look in the glass and study my features dispassionately, as if I were a stranger. There was nothing one could really find fault with, I decided, though my hair was always escaping from clips and hairpins, and the bun at the nape of my neck could never be described as a 'smooth and shining coil' like those of the heroines of romance. What was wrong? Here I was, set down in the centre of everything that was beautiful and romantic, and there was no-one even to hold my hand. One overbold American had tentatively suggested taking me for an expedition into the country, but the idea had been quashed almost before it had been mooted. I think, in any case, Lily Mason had no wish to see me trespass on her preserve.

I shook my head at the image in the glass and then stooped to

71

pick up a couple of hairpins. No, I was fated to be a spinster, growing old and withered in the mean little house beside the tram lines. A dutiful daughter, respected and yet despised.

But youth, and propinquity, and the type of immaturity that makes some older men aware of an urge to mould and idealize were combining to create trouble. An arm slipped through mine as I stood fingering the turquoise trinkets spread on the stall that lined the Ponte Vecchio; a foot touched mine under a table in a restaurant as I tried to twist spaghetti into my laughing mouth; a hand was held out for mine as we climbed amongst the boulders of the olive groves that surrounded the villa, and maintained its clasp, linking me with something of which I was only dimly aware. These were all danger signs. Overnight I had become dynamite without knowing it. The explosion came when Frankie, our childhood troublemaker, arrived for the Christmas holidays.

I had never really had much use for Frankie, but at least he was someone of my own generation, someone with whom I could communicate. And he and I were allowed to go about without the clogging boredom of a chaperone. His mother, surrounded by her circle of dilettante admirers, was, I think, relieved to have us out of the way, and his father desisted from the furtive approaches I have just listed, and which I was finding increasingly difficult to cope with.

Once again things were triggered by a kiss. Only Frankie was more experienced this time. Instead of disappearing, he tried to follow up one sultry situation with another.

'Why did you let me kiss you, then?'

'I didn't,' I shouted into the flaming sunset. 'You're a cad!'

Exchanges of this sort could hardly be ignored or concealed, and so they soon affected the general atmosphere. And then another factor developed – jealousy. All the subtle furtive approaches which probably would have gone no further were suddenly flamed by an older man's frustrated ego.

I was not so naïve as to be unaware of this. For once, I was the centre of attention. But I had no idea how to handle it. When Frankie kissed me that was one thing, but when his father kissed me that was a matter for shame and distress. The night I realized this I pulled on my nightgown, crept into bed, and went to sleep saying 'Hail Mary's' as if I were counting sheep. Things couldn't go on like this was my last conscious thought. And they didn't.

72

That night, tucked up in my bed in the original part of the villa, I was suddenly wakened. The boards in the uncarpeted passage outside were creaking in the stillness. I turned on my side to face the door. I watched the knob slowly turning, and, on a wave of panic, I reached for matches and lit the candle that stood on the bedside table. Slowly, slowly, the door opened, and there, like a beautiful statue in a long white gown, stood Lily Mason. She turned and closed the door, and I sat up to confront her.

The shadowy darkness was black and menacing beyond the feeble reach of the flickering candle. She sat down on my bed and her vivid blue eyes looked into mine. 'Little one,' she said, and her voice held more kindness and concern than accusation, 'this can't go on. You know that, don't you? I need not spell it out. You must leave, before things get out of hand.'

'I know, I know,' I stammered, 'but—'

'But the fact remains that you have upset my two men, and we must think of a way out before more harm is done.'

I felt ashamed and mean, and yet suddenly adult and able to come to terms with the whole sorry business.

8

And that was why I went to stay in the convent at the top of the Spanish Steps. I felt myself to be a fugitive from emotional storms and stresses which I only partly comprehended. I was watched over by Lily Mason's sister, Mother Magdalene Aimée, the gentle nun I had known all my life. How many times as children had Frankie and I eaten a delicious lunch in the convent at Soho (where Mother Magdalene was then), before going to a pantomime or a picture gallery?

Mother Magdalene Aimée never said a word to me, but created the impression that it was the most natural thing in the world for me to be deposited in the convent on the hill. My own mother must have been told the whole story in those days too, but she never said a word about it either, nor asked any questions. Veils were worn with hats, intriguing bits of gauze that revealed as much as they concealed, but the thick veils that shrouded family relationships revealed nothing.

Rome brought me the companionship of other girls, girls from the Convent of the Sacred Heart, with whom I shared exciting, mostly cultural, expeditions. Kathleen O'Connor was my special friend. We would walk up and down the flat roof of the convent, talking and laughing, until the sky turned red and the dome of St Peter's became a black silhouette against the crimson background that changed and faded as we walked and talked.

'Kathleen,' I said one day, 'what makes a nun?'

'I don't know,' she replied.

'I've been trying to find out. A mixture of child and saint, I think, and the mixture varies – sometimes more saint and sometimes more child. And there's something else that is common to them all, like the habit they wear, and I don't know what it is.'

We were sitting in the deserted parlour; portraits of past and present church dignitaries looked down on us from the whitewashed walls, and the polished round table was set out with pious tracts and magazines. 'Here,' I continued, 'in this cold community room, I feel crushed and pulped into a nothing, but when I go into the chapel, I feel there is something I want to do – something waiting for me. Do you think I am getting a vocation?'

'You?' Kathleen laughed. 'You talk as if it was like getting measles. Right now there's romance somewhere.' She pulled a pack of cards out of her coat pocket. 'Shut the door,' she ordered. 'Fortune telling is a sin of some sort.' Gay, inconsequential Kathleen: She pushed aside the papers that had been laid out so neatly on the polished table, and proceeded to deal out cards, with a running commentary on my rose-coloured future. 'There'll be a wedding ring,' she said. 'That's for sure – but not just yet,' and she frowned with concentration. 'There's something in between,' she said; 'a blackness.'

There were two sisters from the neighbouring convent, with whom I also became friends, and after we all returned to England I was invited to stay in their stately home at Dalkeith near Edinburgh. They belonged to one of the oldest Catholic families in England, and their house had its own private chapel where visiting priests celebrated Mass. This was vintage Catholicism, and I responded to its penetrating piety, which gave me a sense of peace.

At the same time, I realized that I would be smothered if I was set down in that rarefied atmosphere for ever. But, for the time being, I was content to absorb new scenes and sensations. I even sat down and embroidered vestments with the two sisters, though I was no needlewoman and would have preferred a walk with the dogs in the lovely countryside. I was also taken to classes in the famous Atholl Crescent School of Cookery in Edinburgh, where we learned to deal with the insides of chickens and plates were called 'ashets'.

I have an idea that Mother Magdalene Aimée was the inspiration behind this visit, intended to set my feet firmly back on the narrow path.

I came home to find new friends among the Freeman family, now removed to a fine big house in Old Road West. By this time Richard Freeman had his own circle of friends and admirers, the hub of which was a family called Standfield, who lived in the solid suburban comfort of the Pelham road. Here, two or three evenings a week, there would be a session of the local doctors and other professional men, including Richard. Jean Standfield, lively and capable, would flit about with tea, coffee and sandwiches. These were male chauvinist evenings as a rule, but Jean knew how to manage men, so they came again and again, and the talk was good and instructive.

Frank Standfield, an engineer by profession, was at that time managing director of Augener, the classical music publishers. Music was another of Richard Austin Freeman's sidelines. We had a small cottage piano bequeathed to my mother when Harry Hamilton 'came down' from Oxford and had no further use for it. When the mood was on him, Richard Freeman would sit down at this piano and a stream of music would trickle from under his fingers, classical music such as Handel and Bach, picked up and stored from sound, for he could not read a note of it.

I have often wondered how my mother felt about this readjustment of the seesaw. Now Richard was way up amongst the stars and she was way down, caught in the trivia of daily worries and petty economies. He was completely independent: he had his own house, his own circle of friends, and his own interests. Her typewriter was the strongest link between them, for she still typed all his work and corrected his proofs. But now she only shared, where once she had possessed.

For me, the Standfield connection added another dimension to a rather meaningless existence. Babs, the eldest of three girls, was four years my junior, but this difference was soon wiped out by the passing months and her maturity of outlook. I was not surprised when eventually she filled her father's shoes and became, herself, managing director of Augener's.

During the summer holidays, in those peaceful days before the motor car took over, the lanes belonged to us and our bicycles. Jean Standfield put up wonderful packed lunches, and off we would go. At the weekends, my brothers joined us. Cuthbert, a graduate of London University, was now a professional soldier, a lieutenant in the gunners. Carteret was serving his apprenticeship as an articled clerk in a firm of accountants, and Gerald was an embryo research chemist. They had all been pushed and helped into meaningful positions. But I was only a girl, no need to plan a career for me; a husband would doubtless drop out of the sky some day.

For a brief period a job did come my way. I became a nurscry governess to the three children of one of my mother's friends: Peggy, Tom and Frank Tolhurst, ages six, seven and nine. We battled with the rudiments of learning in an unorthodox but seemingly satisfactory way. I spun out a story we called the 'Clock Story', collaborating with a gaily coloured cardboard clock with movable hands. We wrote letters to Kim, the old spaniel, and posted them in an oak tree with an inviting hollow in its trunk. We picked wild flowers and pressed them between the leaves of an old dictionary. We collected pebbles, washed them, and used them for demonstrations in arithmetic.

I was whittling time away in this undemanding fashion when I had my first experience of the attentions of a predatory old man. Peggy's grandfather was a widower and looked to me like a grizzly Methusaleh when he collected myself and Peggy in his open carriage to give us a treat. For me, these rides were no fun at all, and even Peggy's childlike face registered her reaction as mutinous acquiescence.

These 'treats' came to an abrupt end when Methusaleh put a withered arm and claw-like hand around my shoulders. I could hardly slap her grandfather's face in front of Peggy, so I flung myself out of the carriage – an easy feat, for the ancient horse was no believer in speed – and made for home across the fields with a sense of outrage and revulsion. Long afterwards a fable grew up that Methusaleh had made an offer of marriage to my parents. Perhaps he did. I shall never know.

At about this time in my life, my mother's eldest brother, Harry, retired and came home from Bermuda. He bought a fine big house with a garden in Bexley, a charming village with an old water mill and a twisting narrow high street, and within cycling distance of Gravesend. Uncle Harry's wife was an outsized Australian, with a flat, kindly face and soft, downy skin, and her brown eyes were always welcoming. She was slow in all her movements, which created a sense of peace when one was with her. They had two sons; one at school, and one who had just started work at the local brewery. It was through this family that I met the Burridges, a widowed mother with two sons and two daughters.

The mother was a big woman, rather like an inflated edition of Queen Victoria, an image she tried to live up to. She would ride through Bexley in an open landau driven by an elderly coachman called Humphrey; one half-expected her to start bowing to right and left, so similar was the image. This travesty of middle-class grandeur delighted me, and a visit to the Burridge family with its good-natured give and take was to be looked forward to, and looked back upon, with vibrant pleasure.

The daughters, Florrie and Daisy, more or less adopted me. I think they sensed my loneliness, even though I myself was not aware of it. Florrie was a clever dressmaker, running up gowns for special occasions on an old Singer sewing machine which was her greatest treasure. I remember one summer when large mushroom-shaped hats were worn. Ruched chiffon was arranged over a wired shape. Florrie made one of these hats for herself and one for Daisy. Then she looked at me sitting on a stool in their bedroom, overawed by these creations. 'And what about you, chick?' she said. 'We can't leave you out.' Then and there she made me a hat that my memory has treasured ever since.

There was an air of jollity about the Burridge household. Their friends dropped in and drifted out again without formality. On impulse, the carpet in the big sitting room would be rolled back, Florrie would sit down at the piano, and her capable fingers would thump out polkas and waltzes, two-steps and tangos, whilst the rest of us danced, light-footed and light-hearted. It was the Burridge family who taught me to dance, and it was Florrie and Daisy who instilled in me enough dress sense so that I began to realize one could not wear a flimsy muslin frock with thick sensible brogues. It was at their house that I met Desmond Nolan.

Like my mother, Mrs Burridge was infatuated by someone she considered a literary genius, a young Dr Lulham who wrote mawkish poetry. I had never met him, but I had listened to her overspill of admiration until rescued by Florrie or Daisy, who had little sympathy with this patron and poet situation. To launch Dr Lulham's first collected volume of poetry, Emily Burridge decided to throw a party.

78

The slim green book with gold leaf lettering had, I suspected, been financed by her. Her daughters had hinted as much, breathing their annoyance into my receptive ears. After all, Richard Austin Freeman was doted on by my mother, so I would know how they felt. Only my mother had picked a winner, and Dr Lulham hardly looked like a sound investment. 'You'll have to come to the wretched party,' coaxed Daisy, 'if it's only to help us bear up.'

So, of course, I went. I bought one of the toques covered with multi-coloured feathers that were all the fashion, though I suspect for older women. For this I coaxed a loan out of old Nanny, who was always good for a 'touch' where I was concerned. Being, as it were, an honorary member of the Burridge family, I went over in the morning and helped the girls cut sandwiches. Their mother directed us, beaming over her three chins and checking the list of guests. Dressed in a purple satin dress trimmed with black lace, her gilded hair piled on top of her head, she might have been a gaudy ceramic goddess.

The big front room was set up with rows of chairs borrowed from the parish hall. At the far end of the room was a small table on which was placed a glass and a carafe of water. Behind it was a high-backed armchair. Here Dr Lulham would be enthroned for the reading of his poems. Another small table held a pile of the green and gold books. 'What some people won't swallow,' muttered Florrie, taking off her apron as the doorbell rang and she went to open the door.

After considerable discussion we had decided to have tea first, in the hope that it would mellow any adverse criticism and help to sell the volumes waiting to be autographed. By the quickness with which our sandwiches, scones and small cakes disappeared, it would seem that the assembling audience had missed out on lunch. Most of them were not-so-young women; a few brought tame-looking husbands. 'Dragged here by the hair, or what's left of it,' Daisy hissed in my ear as we went into the kitchen to refill one of the two big tea pots, also borrowed from the church hall.

'Cook has the day off,' said Florrie. 'I think Mother thought she might give notice.'

Then, into this chattering feminine crowd, walked a big, loose-limbed fellow with a craggy, ugly face and pale blue eyes peering out from behind thick-lensed glasses. The ceramic goddess introduced us. He was obviously a stranger, and I was standing at her elbow when he came up to shake hands. 'Look after Mr Nolan, dear,' she said. 'Introduce him. I must hurry away, as I see Dr Lulham has just arrived.'

'I expect, as you're here, you like poetry,' said Desmond Nolan, awkwardly balancing a cup of tea with a sandwich in his other hand. He pronounced it 'potry' and he spoke in a flat voice with some kind of Irish accent. Not a gentleman by my Aunt Florence's standards, but what did I care – he was obviously attracted, and I might as well get value for the money spent on the toque. So I set my romantic sights on this dour Irishman.

'Oh, yes,' I said, 'I love it, and my hobby is writing it. I like trying out the different forms, rondeaux and roundels and sonnets.'

That was the beginning of a strange courtship, if that is what it was. He told me he was an engineer in the Thames Conservancy Service, and the Conservancy vessel was moored there in the river. 'Why, that's where I live,' I exclaimed – and another link was formed. I forgot that I had been told to introduce him to people. As far as we were concerned, the rest of the afternoon was a vacuum in which two people suddenly found themselves suspended. Dr Lulham, blond and dilettante, wearing a buttonhole carnation which I was quite sure was an Emily Burridge tribute, was escorted by her to his throne at the end of the room. Desmond Nolan sat down beside me. 'We go the same way,' he whispered, as we took our seats. 'May I take you home?'

So we travelled back to Gravesend, in a dingy second-class compartment. He was certainly a solemn sort of companion, which slightly dimmed the picture. Indeed, looking back, I realize that most people would have labelled him boring.

'So you never went to school?'

I shook my head. 'Never, though my aunt, who is a nun, did her best to get me into her school at St Leonard's.'

A frozen look came over his face. 'Then you are—' he paused, as if he found speech difficult. '—you are a Roman Catholic?' There was tension in the air. I felt uncomfortable. He had jerked out the words 'Roman Catholic' almost as if he was making an accusation.

'And what are you?' I asked, feeling the silence hang heavy.

'Presbyterian,' he answered.

I knew little of other beliefs, and Presbyterians I associated with Scotland and thistles. To change the subject I told him, 'I sometimes wish I had gone to school. I can read and write, of course, but I am quite hopeless at arithmetic.'

'That's bad,' he responded. 'Even a woman needs arithmetic for adding up the housekeeping expenses.'

'I suppose I *should* do something about it,' I conceded, 'but I do hate the idea.' The rhythmic rattling of the train took over as we both looked out on the uninspiring sight of Northfleet's cement works.

Just before we drew up to the platform at Gravesend, he leaned across – we were sitting in opposite corners. 'If you like,' he said, 'I will give you lessons in arithmetic. It was my best subject.'

I had not bargained for this. As we walked up the slope from the station, I replied, 'Thank you. I suppose we could try it, but you'll need a lot of patience.'

His craggy face broke into a half-smile. 'We can try it out,' he said, 'if your mother approves.' He took a small notebook out of his pocket. 'I'll give you my address.' He handed me the torn-out page. 'How about next Monday? Let me know.'

'Come in and ask my mother now,' I invited.

But I was relieved when he made some excuse and we said goodbye. My mother was not the sort of person who liked to be taken by surprise. And even by my sophisticated reckoning this was an unusual proposition.

'To teach you arithmetic?' mused my mother, as she lighted one of her Egyptian cigarettes. This was her quiet time: after lunch, sitting in her deep armchair in the small back room that looked out on the balcony, where purple wisteria drooped in untended loveliness. 'I don't see why not. But I had better meet him first.'

So Desmond Nolan became my maths coach, with romance an unexpected extra. We held our sessions in the basement. I resurrected a slate and pencils from my childhood leftovers, a book of tables, and a small volume called *Mathematics for the Beginner*, which I doubt I had ever looked at before. Halfway through our lesson Nanny would appear with cups of tea and biscuits on a small blue plate. I think this interruption was my mother's idea of some kind of chaperonage. But Desmond

81

never tried to flirt; I doubt if he was capable of flirtation. There was a sort of fierce withdrawal if we even touched hands.

Theology would inevitably confuse the issue when we used these breaks to stray from addition and subtraction. He seemed obsessed with the idea of Catholicism as a disruptive force. I countered his thrusts at such issues as indulgences and confession as best I could. But theology, like maths, had never interested me. If I had been older and more experienced, I would have realized that a mind like his, steeped in prejudice from childhood, was immovable.

We sometimes met on other occasions than these lessons in the basement room. There was one subscription dance at the Clarendon Hotel down on the riverfront. He looked strangely out of character in tails and white tie. And his idea of a waltz was more like an Irish jig. Why he came I could never guess, unless it was so that he could hold me so tightly in his arms that it made up for the studied aloofness of our weekly meetings.

Two or three times he came on picnics, making a foursome with Carteret and Babs Standfield. But the light-hearted fun we three erupted into left him cold and puzzled. He had been drawn into an alien world. The 'Noll Bird', the two called him behind his back. And, indeed, he did rather resemble a black crow besieged by twittering, inconsequential sparrows.

Attracted, yet repelled, he seemed unable to claim me or to let me go. As for me, I think I welcomed any situation that I could build up into some form of romance. I was adept at making bricks with a minimum of straw, and then building them into castles in the air.

9

My mother, however, while seemingly indifferent or easy-going where I was concerned, missed little, and had her own way of coping. With what everyone later conceded to be the regrettable and unsuitable Nolan affair dragging on, I was suddenly presented with a month's holiday in Brittany.

'So good for your French,' my mother said. 'Auntie Gertie tells me that the family you are going to speak no English.' So that was it. Aunt Gertie playing the watchful sheepdog again. I made no protests or enquiries. I was so used to having arrangements made for me that life had become a lucky dip; I just plunged my hand into the tub of sawdust and accepted whatever I pulled out.

So one summer day I crossed the choppy blue sea to Brest and found myself one of a homely Breton family in the village of Quimper. They absorbed me into their daily life without fuss; even the tabby cat Imbecile would sit on my lap as if he had known me since he was a kitten. The family consisted of Papa, a rotund little man with a goatee, which at mealtimes he arranged over a napkin tucked round his neck; Marie, the eldest girl, who had a staid youthfulness about her – she had been Papa's housekeeper since her mother died; and Madeleine, the younger sister, a colourless creature who made little impression on me. There was a brother, Jules, who appeared for a few days and serenaded me with 'God Save the King', but with whom I doubt if I exchanged a word. But I was amused at his overt flirtation with Jeanne, the girls' best friend, who spent more time with them than with her widowed mother. And last of all, there was a *bonne à toute faire* who was a superb cook. What she did to the trout of the local river I shall never know, but it is a mouth-watering memory.

I loved the snacks we took when we went walking in the lovely countryside – the slab of dark, slightly bitter chocolate we ate with a hunk of home-baked white bread, washed down with the red wine that was part of our daily life. The girls certainly did their duty by me. They took me to Quimper, where we put black lace veils on our heads and visited the beautiful cathedral. When we came out we stuffed the veils into our picnic basket and roamed round the market place, admiring, but buying little, for we were three penniless people. We picnicked on the beach beyond the oyster beds, and no hotel could have put up a better packed lunch than the *bonne à toute faire* put up for us.

But I did not forget my ugly chunk of humanity as I was meant to do. I wrote him passionate love letters about the beauty of the Breton countryside and the poignancy of unshared ecstasy. 'I sometimes wish it were not so lovely,' I wrote, 'because without you to share it, it gives pain rather than pleasure.' These effusions were never put into the postbox; I wrote them in an old exercise book, and all I sent him were picture postcards.

That he met me at Paddington on my return was a surprise which undid all the hoped-for effects of my exile. In my agitation, I dropped the novel by Anatole France I was holding in one hand as I gripped my shabby pressed-cane case with the other. He took my case from me and said gruffly, in his flat Dublin accent, 'I've missed you. It's been a long time. But there's no need to hurry, we'll have a cup of tea at a little place I know, just round the corner.'

It turned out to be a dull, drab little café, but we had it to ourselves. He was no talker; after that first confession of missing me, he retired into his shell. I think he was, once again, afraid of committing himself. He was drawn, yet repelled by the fact that I was a Sassenach and a Catholic – everything that he had been brought up to dislike and mistrust. That night, I added another letter to the collection in the exercise book. It began, 'Oh my darling, now I know we must break down the barriers. They are only artificial, but our love is real.'

I did not tell my parents of the meeting at Paddington; they just thought my train was late. The sessions in the basement room resumed as if they had never been discontinued. Only now there was more awareness of the basic reason for these meetings, and the accidental touch of a hand set off sparks. Then, suddenly, the whole impossible situation came down to one moment of decision.

Desmond came along one day, and, as he sat down beside me, he pushed away the collection of books and pencils. He turned and gripped my hands in his so fiercely that it hurt. 'This can't go on,' he said, in a strange, harsh voice. 'You've got to choose between me and the papacy and all it stands for.' He let go of my hands and took an official-looking envelope out of his pocket. 'I've been offered a job in South Africa. Come with me. We can be married out there. No priest, no promises, no holy water.'

There was a strange, fanatical light in his pale blue eyes. I was too stunned to speak. 'You're the only one I've ever wanted to marry,' he continued, 'but I could not marry a Roman Catholic – could not or would not, it comes to the same thing. Give it all up. One of us has to give way, and it would not cost you what it would cost me.' That last assertion was true enough. Years after I realized how true, with the ugliness of Northern Ireland.

As he finished his outburst, I shook my head. The pain of my denial shot through me. 'No, no, I can't give up my faith, even for – for love.'

'I should have known,' he said bitterly. 'I should never have looked your way.' There was a moment of stricken silence and then he stood up and pulled me up with him. 'I'll take this for a memory,' he said, and his kiss was like the sealing of a fierce despair. When he shut the door, I knew that he had shut me out of his life, and I laid my head down on the table and wept.

And that was how old Nanny found me. She sat beside me and drew my head close to her warm, safe bosom. 'He was too old for you, Miss Dolly. Too old and no fun in him. It wouldn't have lasted. God knows best, and the Pope was a pill he would never have swallowed – Black Protestants they call them in Ireland.'

For weeks I rebelled against fate, but gradually a sense of martyrdom replaced the cold fact of renunciation. My sense of drama obscured the feeling of personal loss: I was a martyr who had given up a human love for the faith. Once more I turned to the poets for consolation. I propped my *Oxford Book of Verse* up on a pillow while I made my bed, and wrote poems about love and renunciation.

Where was I drifting? What was I going to do? Why should my brothers have found answers to such questions? But now the mysterious 'blackness' silly Kathleen had predicted in the convent was beginning to descend. Rumours of war were seeping into our thoughts and conversations. We shut our eyes and put our fingers into our ears, but apprehension was in the very air we breathed.

Cuthbert, a lieutenant in the gunners, gathered the four of us together in a London teashop. This was to be a discussion of our summer holiday.

'Let's forget it all on the Norfolk Broads,' he suggested. 'We're going to be scattered from now on; if war comes, as I'm sure it must, we'll all be in it. But for two weeks we'll forget it all,' he said, 'and go sailing on the Broads. We'll take books and the old gramophone with us.'

He looked across the table at me. 'Perhaps it will mean escape for you,' he told me, 'but it will be hell for the rest of us.'

10

And so, in the June of 1914, we chartered a white-sailed boat and went wandering along the rivers of East Anglia.

I was told that I was the cook, and I stared with distrust at a terrifying Primus stove that stuttered and protested when Carteret got it going for a cup of tea. The rest of the equipment consisted of a saucepan and a frying pan that showed signs of previous misuse. But to be shut up with that stove in a small galley was a real test of courage.

Day by day we threaded our way in and out of the intricate waterways where the tall reeds rustled in the breeze that filled our sails and water hens scuttled in and out of the beds. Men in flat-bottomed boats ruthlessly cut back the reeds, but their gentle rustling was the last thing we heard at night when we moored our craft to the bank.

In those days there was solitude and quiet to be found on the Broads if you looked for it, but once or twice we hitched our boat to a small landing stage and shared the music of a gramophone, singing, talking, and laughing with strangers with whom we could communicate because we were sharing the magic of enchanted waters.

'Norwich tomorrow,' said Cuthbert, as our first week drew to a close. He helped himself to another slice of ham. 'We'll buy some bloody meat there. Ham washed down with tea or cider is all very well, but enough really is enough.'

But Norwich had more than steak waiting for us. It had trouble, starting with a niggling pain in my uncharted interior – pain that persisted until the whole of me seemed aflame. Groaning, my knees drawn up to my chin, I could find no escape. The young doctor Cuthbert fetched, questioned and prodded and gave a welcome jab with a needle.

I had appendicitis. Appendicitis was fashionable. Harley Street had been busy diagnosing it for its wealthy patients ever since the coronation of Edward VII had been postponed because of it. I was rushed up to London, and that night found me a patient in the hospital of St John and St Elizabeth, where I first got a glimmering of what I wanted to do with my life.

I had never known any kind of routine before and the hospital was my first experience of organized caring. The orderly sequence of the duties of night and day fascinated me, even though I myself was caught up in the ruthless machinery. It was the not knowing that scared me. Horrible visions flitted through my ignorant mind. I felt as though I could have died of fear but for the comforting hand of Sister Teresa slipped into mine as we went down in the lift. I can see her rosy cheeks and blue eyes now, as she looked down on me. 'It's just like going to sleep,' she said. 'Say one Hail Mary and you're off. And when you wake up, you won't believe you've had an operation.'

I had been through the ordeal. The lonely and frightened – they belonged to me. To be wakened at five in the morning and told to wash myself after a night broken by strange noises and happenings might have put some people off, yet not me. My bare feet were on the floor boards as soon as my stitches were out, and I was trying to help, even if it was only with words.

'I want to be a nurse,' I told my mother when I returned home. But the words died on my lips when I saw the expression on her face.

'You are much too delicate for that sort of life,' she responded adamantly. Perhaps her attitude would have extinguished my enthusiasm for ever, but for the forces of war closing in on us.

The third of August, 1914. We could no longer pretend we were deaf and blind. Across the Channel all hell had been let loose, and with the over-running of Belgium, our hospitals began to take in the wounded men from the defeated army. Gertrude Pinching, whose husband was a consultant at the local hospital, came to enlist me amongst her volunteer nursing aides.

'Talk my mother into letting me help,' I whispered as I opened the door. 'She will listen to you.'

My mother was sitting in her armchair, sipping her afternoon cup of China tea and smoking an Egyptian cigarette. 'Fetch another cup, darling,' she ordered. I sought out Nanny in the basement.

'Nanny,' I said, sitting on the floor at her feet, 'I want to be a nurse more than anything.'

'It's a hard life, Miss Dolly, and your Ma thinks you're too delicate.'

'Rubbish,' said I, 'it's a fable, and you know it.'

And then suddenly Gertrude Pinching was calling softly from the top of the stairs. 'Come up, it's all fixed.'

The next day I reported at the local hospital for my first tour of duty. Space was limited, equipment makeshift, yet as I took a cotton overall from a peg in the matron's office, I felt elation and confidence which were hardly justified by my performance. But the cot cases were not many, and the trained staff took care of them. We volunteers cut and buttered bread, brewed tea, handed out washing bowls; we looked sympathetically at snapshots of mothers and sweethearts, and we did our best to restore some measure of hope to the hopeless. 'Of course this war will be over by Christmas,' we assured them.

The mud of Flanders. My mind holds another picture, a steaming bath filled with hot soapy water and disinfectant. Into this we threw their socks, and I shall never forget the slime and smell of that tub. But this was service, I told myself.

I also rolled bandages and made sandbags at the local Red Cross centre. I was the only girl roped in for these activities, which I shared with the elderly and the rather mindless type of housewife. After a trial period, thoughts of enlisting in the VAD (Voluntary Aid Detachment) began to gather impetus. My restlessness erupted in a letter to Aunt Florence, who could always be relied upon to cut corners if she chose. 'I believe in going to the top,' she would say. In my case the top was Lady Perrot of the Red Cross.

One morning, in the summer of 1915, I stood on the platform at Gravesend station, waiting for the 'up' train. In my hand was a letter of introduction to Lady Perrot. As the train drew near, I heard a voice behind me. 'Hello. What are you doing here?' The voice that spoke was Destiny; Destiny with all the appearance of a very ordinary young woman wearing a muslin frock and a floppy hat. She was a cousin, temporarily living in rooms in the town. Her husband was fighting 'somewhere' in France, and she was waiting for a job in the War Office.

She followed me into a third-class compartment, though I'm

certain her own ticket was for second class. As the train slowly chugged and halted its way to London, I told her of my resolve to become a VAD. She shook her head. 'Don't. They are falling over themselves, getting in the way. Do the thing properly. Train as a nurse in one of the teaching hospitals. This war is not going to end tomorrow; three years of training will make you an asset, whichever way it goes.'

I was silent. Her words exactly echoed my own secret conviction. She looked out of the window at the dingy, smoke-grimed houses that had replaced the bright gardens and neat villas of suburbia. 'We'll get to Waterloo in about five minutes,' she said. 'How about it?' She turned to me, and my answer came short and decisive.

'Yes,' I said, 'you are right. But what do I do now? Where do I go?' Panic seized me.

'We'll take a taxi to University College Hospital; one of the honoraries is a friend of my father's. I'll arrange for you to see the matron, and then I'll disappear, and good luck to you.'

So we did just that, and she left me sitting in an ugly little room opposite a door marked Matron's Office. It was very quiet in that little room, but outside feet passed up and down the corridor, purposeful feet that had work to do in this imposing building. There was the faint whiff of ether in the air, stirring up memories of my days in St John and St Elizabeth.

Then the door opened, and there stood the woman who would control my comings and goings for the next three years. She might have stepped straight out of a Rembrandt portrait. Dressed in black, her pale face framed by a white crimped cap, she was at once a symbol of authority. 'You wished to see me.' It was a statement rather than an enquiry.

'Yes – yes, please, Matron,' I stammered.

'Then come into my office.' I followed her into a small, dingy room, feeling raw and countrified before this unheralded majesty. Quite a human smile flitted across the impassive mask. She seated herself behind her desk and indicated that I was to sit in the chair opposite. 'Why do you wish to train as a nurse?'

I hesitated. Answering the question was not as simple as it sounded. I did not want to sound smug and self-righteous. 'Because I wanted to do something worthwhile, and I feel I would like to look after people and learn to do it properly.'

'I see.' Very noncommittal, I thought uneasily. The august

figure leaned down and opened a drawer in the desk. 'Here is a copy of our rules and regulations. Take them home and read them carefully.' The quiet voice went on explaining, elaborating. Finally, I was told, 'You will start with a salary of eight pounds per annum, paid monthly. This will be increased annually. You will get your final certificate at the end of your third year. You may then, if you wish, pay the hospital the sum of thirty pounds and leave as a trained nurse. Or you can stay on for a fourth year and qualify in massage or midwifery.'

The question of payment had not even entered into my considerations, so the amount neither shocked nor surprised me. In any case, the word exploitation was, at that time, well and truly overlaid by the words vocation and dedication. 'When you have filled in the application form,' the voice continued, 'send it to me, and if I find everything satisfactory, I will send you instructions as to uniform and the date you will start your training.'

'Thank you, Matron,' I said, and took the papers she held out to me. Judging the interview to be over, I got up to go. Instinctively I backed out of the small drab room as if I were in the presence of royalty. That gesture was my first acceptance of the rigid etiquette that was to rule my life for the next three years. As I descended the stone stairway I thought how unreal it all seemed. Was I really proposing to spend the next three years in this imposing building, with its rather dumpy little woman as a figurehead?

I went home that evening in a state of frightened elation, having made, for the first time in my life, a major decision on my own. I was met with a wet blanket of disapproval. 'You are not strong enough for a nurse's training,' objected my mother. She must have been thinking of the salad bowl christening. Aunt Gertie was dubious: 'I hope you'll be able to go to Mass on Sunday,' she wrote, when she heard the news. She knew University College Hospital had been founded by an Anglican sisterhood. (She was right. Formal observance was squeezed out of my life by the crowded, energy-absorbing system that was a nurse's training then.) Nanny was more encouraging. 'Nothing venture, nothing have. You're wasted here, just pottering about.'

I kissed Nanny's cheek. Even now she meant security. Jerked out of my middle-class complacency by a world war, I looked to her for comfort. And then it came, the letter from the Matron of University College Hospital. For the next three years I would be learning to submerge my own ego; learning to live at ease in an institution run by women; I, who had never even been to school, learning the skills of nursing. I had been accepted as a probationer nurse. The way was clear. At last my life had meaning.

Part Three
The War Years

11

One golden October day in 1915, I stood on the steps of the New Nurses' Home in Huntley Street. 'My home or my prison?' I wondered, as I rang the bell. Waiting there with my shabby, bulging suitcase, I felt tingling excitement take over from apprehension. I was facing up to a challenge, and I would carry it through, somehow, to fulfilment. My thoughts rushed to and fro. I was a Londoner now. I had left behind all my country freedoms: the bicycle that had opened out the beauty of the Kentish countryside; the timeless dreaming under the great trees in Cobham Woods; the rhyming dictionary with its worn covers, for poetry would no longer colour my waking life. It would be a much grimmer reality from now on.

The great hospital that was to swallow me up for three, perhaps four, years stood within a few minutes walk of Euston Station. The traffic from Gower Street and the Tottenham Court Road roared past continuously – almost day and night, I imagined, as I stood on the doorstep in Huntley Street, which linked the two great thoroughfares. All around the turreted, red-brick building were the slums that housed my future patients: derelict buildings with broken windows patched with brown paper; dreary women in tattered clothes, peeling potatoes and gossiping on the worn and dirty steps of what had been the town houses of the rich and fashionable; ragged, barefoot children playing, fighting, and yelling. One day I would meet many of them in Casualty, sitting on the worn, scrubbed benches, loved and cared for by Sister Jane.

The door of the Nurses' Home was opening. My racing thoughts were stilled by the appearance of a smart, uniformed maid who was looking me up and down. 'You'll be the new nurse,' she said. 'Follow me.' An elderly porter was standing in the hall beside the lift gates. 'Here, George, take the new nurse's luggage up to Room 64,' ordered my guide. He nodded sullenly, as if this task was the ultimate vexation in a world already dismal from every point of view.

The pert little maid opened a door labelled 'Home Sister'. She led me into a small, unwelcoming room and left me there, closing the door without a word. The decor was a mixture of varnished brown paint, accented by walls of a dull, repellent green. I had started to read a notice instructing me what to do in case of fire when the door opened and an angular figure in dark blue uniform walked in. Her solid waist was clasped by a silver buckled belt, from which dangled a bunch of keys. 'I am the Home Sister,' she said. 'Sister Miriam, who is usually in charge, is away. I hope you will be happy here, Nurse Bishop. Now come with me.'

A faint fluttering of the servility that is born of rigid etiquette turned my 'Yes, Sister' into a nervous squeak. As we went up in the lift I was warned, 'Will you please note that this lift is not for the use of probationer nurses.' 'Yes, Sister,' I squeaked again. On the fourth floor the creaking lift bumped to a stop. Sounds of laughter came from two or three of the rooms opening on to the long corridor, and a figure in knickers and camisole disappeared like a flash.

Room 64. A square cell furnished with a chest of drawers with a mirror on top, a hard, cane-bottomed chair, and a grey rug beside a narrow bed covered with a white cotton spread. After informing me that someone would fetch me for tea in half an hour and giving me a few words to prepare me for my first assignment, Sister shut the door behind her and left me in a state of very mixed feelings.

Tears gathered as I bent over my case and opened it. I pulled a handkerchief out of the pocket of my dress and wiped my eyes. There, on top, lay the uniform so proudly packed by Nanny only a few short hours ago. I laid it, piece by piece, upon the bed. Long butcher-blue dress, the bodice boned and buttoning down the front; bibbed and starched apron; 'Sister Dora' cap, its wide starched band turned back from the face; stiffly starched collar, cuffs and belt. Oh, where were all the studs I had to put in these items! My nervous fingers pushed them through the stiff slits until I was scarlet-faced and almost at a screaming point. Then a knock came. 'Come in,' I invited, longing to say, 'Go away. I'm finished. I can't go on with this.'

The probationer who had been sent in to fetch me gave me a

Dorothy aged eight

Dorothy aged five, with
Cuthbert aged four and
Carteret, two

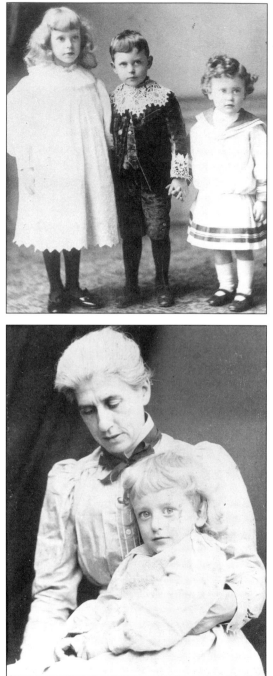

Nanny with Gerald

Alice Bishop with her children: Carteret, Gerald, Cuthbert and Dorothy

Dorothy's father, Bernard Edmonson Bishop

A view of the house in Constitution Crescent, Gravesend

The 'mean little house' in Clarence Place, Gravesend

Babs Standfield, Carteret,
Gerald and Dorothy on a picnic

Desmond Nolan, Babs
Standfield and Carteret

Aunt Florence and Aunt Gertie

Above left: Gerald, Cuthbert and Carteret in 1914. This is the photograph Dorothy took with her to University College Hospital

Above right: Dorothy's final certificate from University College Hospital

A newspaper clipping of Oliver Moriarty

Dorothy on the roof of
the Anglo-American
Hospital, Cairo, 1921

Engagement in Cairo

Oliver and Dorothy on their honeymoon, 1922

Dorothy and the car at the entrance to the flat in Cairo, soon after her marriage to Oliver

pitying glance as I paused to adjust my cap in the mirror. 'Moor it with a pin,' she said, 'we all do,' and she handed me one from her own cap. She little guessed what courage this simple act gave me.

My cap secure, we walked along a flagged passage into the vast underworld of the steamy hospital kitchens. Through the haze I saw hurrying, white-coated people. The air was heavy with the lingering smells of countless meals. Great copper pans hung on the walls.

Beyond the kitchen was the nurses' dining room. The babble of talk was alarming, but more frightening was the assessing silence as we entered. For a few brief moments, I, the new probationer, held the stage. I was seen, appraised and forgotten as the chatter once more picked up its volume. My guide pushed me into a vacant chair and dumped a cup of strong but tepid tea in front of me. Someone else pushed bread, margarine, and a wartime recipe of plum and apple jam towards me. I sipped the tea and nearly choked on the bread and jam in my anxiety to catch up with the others.

'Are you ready, Nurse?' I jumped up; the brief interlude for tea was over. There was a general exodus, but I felt lost in this purposeful crowd. Then someone touched my arm. 'You are to come to Ward 8, Men's Medical,' she said. 'I'm the senior probationer there, and Dagge is my name.' In those days you learned as you worked. We were pushed into a ward without any preliminary teaching. Some of us had never seen a bedpan or urinal. 'Sink or swim' was the unspoken motto. Most of us did learn to swim, but it was a hard struggle.

I meekly followed Dagge through the heavy swinging doors of Ward 8, which closed with a clash behind us. The Sister, who was writing at her desk, looked up. She said nothing and resumed her writing – a silent rebuke for letting the door slam. I summoned all the courage I had and approached the desk to stammer out an apology. The seated figure went on writing. Without lifting her head, she said in clear, staccato tones, 'Nurse Dagge, will you instruct the new probationer in some of her duties?' It was my first violation of hospital etiquette. No probationer should ever address a Sister directly.

After this, as far as Sister was concerned, I might not have existed. I felt rejected and humiliated. I was also aware of an audience. Heads popped up from pillows as I walked down the polished strip of parquet flooring between the rows of beds, twelve on each side. I followed Dagge into the small ward kitchen. 'Don't look like a tragedy queen,' she told me. 'Take off your cuffs, and put on your sleeves – or haven't you got them with you? Never mind, here is a spare pair.' She opened the kitchen drawer and held up a pair of the half-sleeves with which we replaced our cuffs when we came on duty. 'Sink room next,' she said. 'We'll be doing washings in a few minutes.'

On one side of the sink room were shelves for the urine bottles and bedpans, which were shaped like banjos and had hollow handles. Dagge showed me a pile of linen bedpan covers and a big bag filled with tow (jute fibre). 'Don't forget to stuff some tow in the handles,' she instructed. Then, seeing my look of incredulity, she laughed. 'This is a hospital, not a nursing home. We scrape along and do the best we can. Don't look shocked. They do have toilet paper in the private wards.'

There was an overpowering smell of Jeyes fluid and carbolic acid in this unsavoury room. The big flushing unit shared a wall space with a sink serviced by hot and cold water. I was thinking it would be hard to keep a sense of vocation in this unlovely setting when Dagge nudged me. 'Here, we don't stand still and we don't sit down; we have to be seen moving, doing things all the time. Take one of those basins, fill it with hot water, and take it to old Daddy in Bed 8.'

The old man in Bed 8 had his head tied up in a red bandanna. Twinkling red-rimmed blue eyes looked out from a hairy face like a bird's nest. His grey flannel shirt (all the men wore grey flannel shirts) matched his beard in colour. ''ere Nurse, you just get the doings from me locker – soap and flannel and sich-like – and I'll wash the old dial meself. You can 'op it and look after some of them 'elpless fellers,' he ordered cheerfully, as I set the basin down on top of the locker.

Bedmaking, which followed washings, was a nightmare of precision and coordinated effort. I tugged and pulled and tweaked blankets and sheets in a frantic attempt to keep pace with the senior staff. Her patience ran out when she looked up at the big round clock that hung over the door of every ward, a silent reminder that a nurse's life is a sustained attempt to squeeze the work of twenty-four hours into twelve. Time had been a pleasant friend until now, but at this moment it seemed to have changed into an enemy. I tucked the corners of the last bed with a neat finish born of despair. No comment from Nurse Martin, and I gave a sigh of relief for this.

When the last bed was made, I straightened up and looked around. Dagge appeared, wheeling a trolley. 'I have to go to the kitchen for milk,' she told me cheerfully, 'so you take the suppers round. And, for heaven's sake, don't give beef tea to the gastrics.'

'But how am I to know which are the gastrics?' I wailed.

'Come down into the kitchen, and I'll show you the list of special diets. Take down their numbers.' Dagge was, at heart, a kindly girl, but the pressures on a probationer were apt to squeeze out the impulse to do anyone a favour. It was a case of every girl for herself and let Sister catch the hindmost.

That first day (it seemed more like a year, so packed was it with facts, impressions, fears) came to an end at last. Cleaning up the sink room was the final battle against time. I felt that I had been steeped in Jeyes fluid as I hung the last of the rubber sheets I had scrubbed on the rail to dry. As I returned the last of the sputum mugs to its owner's locker top, I hoped Dagge had not noticed the revulsion on my face when she first dumped them in front of me to be emptied.

Like most dreamers faced with grim reality, I was weary and disillusioned as I closed the doors of Ward 8 behind me and joined the stream of nurses on their way to second supper. But I also felt that life had taken on new meaning. Before I undressed that night, I set the photograph of my three brothers – taken in those first frantic weeks of war – on top of my chest of drawers. I looked proudly at the three khaki-clad figures, all doing their bit in conditions far worse than I would ever know. I would give them no cause to be ashamed of me. I was in the war effort now, and I would stick it out.

12

'Five past six, Nurse.' With a long, shuddering sigh, I woke the next morning to reality. Like a mechanical figure that has had its spring released, I tumbled out of bed. Rap, rap, rap. Up and down the corridor. 'Five past six, Nurse.' Miraculously, I was dressed in time to join my fellow workers on their way to the dining hall. The homely smell of kippers as we passed through the kitchens made me realize how hungry I was. In the middle of the hall was a round table. 'For us, the pros,' whispered Dagge, as she took my arm and led me to it.

Punctually, at a quarter to seven, the little bright-eyed Night Sister closed the doors and sat down to preside at the head of the long refectory table. My attention was divided between my kipper and the scene before me. Now the seniors began to dribble in; the seasoned sinners who hoped an 'Excuse me, Sister' would be the only price to pay for those precious extra minutes in bed.

We ate swiftly. There was little talk, for most of us were hardly awake. We gulped down our tea, hoping it would rouse our sluggish awareness that the day's work was about to start. Overhead, under the great skylights, chirped the sparrows, the invincible little birds that I was always to associate with that dining hall.

Breakfast was followed by 'posting'. Night Sister got up and announced the day's changes. There was a pregnant silence as she passed along the lines of seated nurses, each one wondering 'Will I be moved?' To my relief I was to go to Ward 8 again. At least I would not feel utterly lost.

Night Sister returned to the head of the long table and we all stood up to say grace, with a backing from the sparrows, who would soon swoop down into the deserted hall to pick up their daily crumbs. Following grace, we pulled out our chairs and knelt down to recite the simple morning prayers we had known from childhood. I found it strangely moving, as if it united and strengthened our common purpose. With the concluding 'Amen' we got up, pushed our chairs back into place, and drifted out of the hall towards our appointed wards.

Our way lay through draughty underground passages and then, finally, up the spiral of the great central staircase where the 'scrubbers' were busy with buckets and mops. Shapeless figures in shabby overalls, with swollen hands and noses red from the cold which poverty made their portion. Ill-nourished specimens from the slums and tenements that surrounded us, women thankful to earn a few miserable shillings a week. Conscious of hot tea and kipper inside me, I felt a sudden rush of pity. This was the first time I had seen evidence of poverty, real poverty; this sort of human misery I had met only in the pages of Dickens.

We came to Ward 8, with the red screens drawn across the doors, the 'closed ward' sign. 'Good morning, Nurse,' came from all but the very sick as we walked up the ward. They welcomed us; we were important to them. My sense of vocation returned.

The ward kitchen seemed to be full of people who had no use for me. Bridie, a cross-eyed maid, was grumbling at the night nurses and calling on heaven to save her from the invading day nurses. I turned to Dagge as she opened the drawer where the sleeves were kept. 'What am I to do?' I humbly asked.

'Put screens around Daddy 8,' she instructed. 'Give him a good going over, and don't forget it's doctors' day.'

And just what does that mean, I wondered, as I lugged the heavy screens across the ward. Daddy 8 would soon enlighten me. 'It's the day the big boss comes round with his young men, and they prods you here and there and talks about yer innards as if you was a bloomin' dummy.' He chuckled knowingly. I pulled off his grey flannel shirt and started to soap his hairy old chest, whilst he wheezed protestingly. 'I don't hold wiv all this soap and water lark,' he sputtered, as I dabbed at his face with a square of flannel. 'All very well for babies, but the likes of me is best wivout it.'

Dagge showed her rosy face round the screen. She dumped a bottle labelled 'waste ether' on a corner of the locker. 'That stuff!' snorted Daddy. 'Pure pison, I calls it. Stinkin' pison.'

'What do I do with it?' I enquired meekly.

'Well, first you cuts me toenails, then you soaks some cotton wool in it and pokes around me toes. Smells 'orrible, so it does.'

In between the hairy old chest and the toes, there was a problem area to be dealt with. Daddy's shrewd old eyes noted my Victorian embarrassment. He said gently, and with a delicacy I shall never forget, 'Leave the rest to me, Nurse. Just 'and me the towel and the flannel. The likes of me has to help out the likes of you.'

Coming back from two hours off duty (ten till twelve), I found everyone lined up for the distribution of dinners. Sister, a large iron spoon in one hand, stood at one end of the long central table which was spread with a white cloth. She was like a conductor of an orchestra standing ready. Then a sweating porter staggered in, carrying a great copper serving dish which he dumped down in front of her. In a few minutes he returned with a similar dish, full of potatoes. Bridie, the cross-eyed maid who stood beside Sister, started peeling the potatoes with the speed and efficiency of a machine. Rough and ready indeed, judging by the hospital meals of today.

When the porter put the third dish, which held fish, in front of Sister, she started to wield her serving spoon, filling up the plates with appropriate portions, while Dagge and I hurried up and down the ward with laden trays. I found myself muttering, 'Fish for Bed 1, mince for Bed 2,' and then I panicked. 'Bed 6 says he wants fish, Sister.'

'I should hope he does.' Sister glared at me. 'I sent fish to Bed 6.' Her eyes were like glittering pebbles.

'Yes, Sister.' The squeak had returned to my treacherous voice.

And so it went, good patches and bad patches, learning the hard way, but learning. Painful step by painful step, I was gaining ground. I was released for first dinner, which meant that I escaped the bedpan round that followed dinners in the ward. In the dining room, hashed mutton was being dished out with a very sparing hand, for meat was rationed. It was served with glutinous rice and followed by watery custard.

At twenty minutes to two the presiding Sister rose. 'For what we have received, may the Lord make us truly thankful,' she intoned, and we agreed with muted amens, for we were still conscious of a desire for second helpings. We went back to our wards to relieve those left on duty for the second sitting in the dining hall. We had to tidy beds and locker tops in preparation for the weekly visiting hour.

'Nurse Bishop.' My heart stood still. What could have gone wrong? 'Remove that orange pip from the top of Bed 5's locker, at once.' Yes, there it was, an orange seed that seemed to have swelled to the size of an ostrich egg. I seized the bowl and rushed to remove the offending object. 'Nurse Bishop, it's inexcusable to run, except in a case of fire or haemorrhage.' My nerveless fingers let go of the bowl, which fell with a clatter that went on and on. My nursing career was over! I stood over the fallen bowl like someone turned to stone.

But visiting days had their own problems. Many of our patients were gastric ulcer cases on special and restricted diets. Their relatives were firmly convinced that, for some obscure reason, their loved ones were being deliberately starved. It was the duty of Dagge and myself to stand at the ward doors, take any parcels brought by the visitors, and put them on the kitchen table for Sister's inspection.

''Ere, dearie,' one old woman said to me as she handed me a lump of something wrapped in newspaper, 'our Dad do love 'is bit o' pickled pork. No need to show it to Sister, just a bit o' understanding 'tween you and me, see.' 'Our Dad,' of course, was an acute gastric ulcer patient.

The visitors had gone and the ward was settling back into its routine, when the junior staff held out a jar filled with carbolic, in which were immersed half a dozen thermometers, and asked, 'Can you take temperatures, Nurse?' I should have answered 'No,' but, full of hope, I answered 'Yes.' I took a thermometer out of the jar, wiped off the carbolic, and prepared to tackle Bed 1. He was another old man with a bird's nest face, out of which jutted a big hooked nose. His veined and bony hand lay expectantly on top of the bed clothes. His sunken eyes looked challengingly at me.

'They orfen 'as trouble findin' that there pulse o' mine,' he informed me proudly. I inserted the thermometer under the leathery tongue before I picked up the bony hand. I was conscious of a sardonic look of amusement in his hooded glance. I pulled the Ingersoll watch out of the pocket in my uniform. I could feel the beating of my own heart, but in that

103

bony wrist no flutter of life. My nervous fingers played a searching tattoo whilst the knowing eyes gave out the message, 'I told you so.' Then, just as I was about to give up, I found it, thready and uncertain, but a pulse. It seemed a miracle.

13

With a week or two of experience behind me, some things got easier. I discovered that bedmaking could be quite a relaxing affair – we used this time to gossip over the recumbent forms of our patients, and sometimes they chipped in with interested comments. The patients had been wonderful, helping with their hints when possible. Bed 16, a pale young man with pebble-lens glasses who was convalescent, was always ready to lend a hand when Sister was out of the ward. His 'Sister's got the rats, look out, Nurse,' was like a gale warning; we trimmed our sails, and kept out of the storm centre.

But mostly the training was difficult, and only the dedicated, or tough, survived. The status barriers did not make life easier. We were very grade conscious, and senior probationers seldom made friends with juniors. I was lucky, for amongst my contemporaries I found three friends, and kept them through my years of training and beyond.

Symonds was the eldest and most senior, a former school-teacher caught up in the war effort. She reminded me of the wooden Dutch dolls found in every little girl's toy cupboard. She had rosy cheeks, bright blue eyes, and black hair, smoothed and parted in the middle, then drawn into a tight bun.

Maxwell was Scottish; there was breeding in every line of her serious, aristocratic face.

Wharton, the youngest, was a plump, motherly little thing, never happy unless she was fussing over someone. It was Wharton who usually made the cocoa over a small spirit stove when we had our almost nightly meetings. It was Wharton who produced cake or biscuits, handing this treat round as we squatted on the floor, wrapped in our white bedspreads, like a group of snowmen because the New Nurses' Home had no heating.

In the Old Home, attached and part of the main hospital building, there were gurgling radiators and gas rings for the heating of drinks. Pass your first exam, put on the striped dress of a staff nurse, and you transferred to these Elysian comforts.

All ranks of nurses shared the sitting room. Its chief attraction was that it was warm, and in it was housed a shabby upright piano. Here Home Sister gave her lectures, seated at the centre table, where we probationers were gathered, pencils poised over notebooks. The Sister Tutor of today would hardly recognize the academic value of these lectures. They dealt mainly with protocol, the basics of bandaging and splint-making, and very elementary physiology. To help with this subject, Sister produced a figure we called the China Lady. She was fitted with hooks on which were hung the vital organs. There was also a box of bones, shiny and well polished from the handling by the seekers of knowledge, who used them as a macabre sort of jigsaw puzzle.

Up in the clinical theatre on the top floor Jimmy the Skeleton swung on his chain, and it was here that the honoraries gave their lectures to the students and nurses. But, unlike our modern counterparts, our knowledge was bought dearly, with our own time as likely as not. Indeed, our off-duty time was very often at risk.

Looking back, I realize what a very small world was that of a probationer nurse. Outside the red-brick walls of our hospital, across the English Channel, a war was raging. And yet, except when one of our menfolk came home on leave, or a Zeppelin raid robbed us of sleep, or there was the name of someone we knew in the casualty lists, we were smothered in trivia that obscured the larger issues – the war, with all its far-reaching consequences, and the continuing fight for women's suffrage.

For we were beginning to feel the birth pangs of a new era. War was destroying, but also creating. A new society was in the making. Women everywhere were starting to assert their rights to equality. How did I feel about it? What did I think? The truth is, I thought very little about it. When Mrs Pankhurst had been in and out of prison, I barely noted the fact. My teenage mind was more concerned with poetry than politics.

And now this issue seemed less important than ever. Certainly, my three friends and I never discussed women's suffrage. We were far more concerned with happenings within the four walls of University College Hospital; and in those days there was no radio or television to stimulate our interest, and who had time to read the papers?

There was one experience, though, that even the most junior probationer could not escape, and that was direct contact with death, the invisible enemy that every nurse is trained to fight.

Two weeks after I entered University College Hospital, there was a death on my side of the ward. We came on duty one morning to find three screens shutting off Bed 2 from the ward's activities. Just inside those screens the night staff and the night Sister were conferring. Through the muted sounds of ward routine broke the harsh syncopation of the rattling breaths of a dying man.

Dagge and I went into the kitchen. Bridie greeted us. 'Poor old Daddy 2, 'e's 'ad 'is. The fourth in six weeks,' she added. 'It's them fogs, they're killing, that's what they are, to them as is bronchials.' With a gusty sigh she poured herself out a cup of tea from a pot just made by the night pro.

Dagge looked at me, and my feelings must have been evident, for she said, 'Cheer up, you'll get used to it.'

She sauntered over to adjust her cap in the mirror hanging on the side of the dresser. 'The first week I was here, we had four deaths in three days,' she told me over a shoulder. 'That broke me in good and proper,' she added. I said nothing. I had to pull myself together, face up to the inescapable. I had to conquer the primitive fear that had taken hold of me.

I followed Dagge into the sink room and filled a basin with hot water, then carried it to the patient in Bed 4. He was a cheerful little Cockney. ''Is number's nearly up, Nurse,' he said, and jerked a thumb in the general direction of Bed 2. 'Poor ole geezer. Feet foremost, that's the way 'e'll go ahter this ward.' Not a callous comment, only a fact stated with a touch of pity.

The work of the ward went on – the washings, bedmaking, and the usual gossip over the recumbent forms – but in a subdued key, with no joking comments, waiting for the black cloud to roll away. And through it all I was fearfully aware of the rattling breaths and the hiss of the oxygen cylinder.

Then, as I handed a mug of milk to the patient in Bed 6, the painful breathing ceased, the oxygen tap was turned off. This was it, I told myself. The staff nurse summoned me. 'Nurse Bishop, will you help Nurse Layng.'

Nurse Layng was behind those red cotton screens. My reserves of courage were at a very low ebb, but I pulled myself together and did as I was told. Nurse Layng, her gentle, bespectacled face flushed with the effort, was struggling to remove pillows. The sight of the dead man's head lolling and rolling as in gruesome protest nerved me to action and I grabbed a shoulder. The feel of the still-warm flesh as I pulled off the grey flannel shirt, the sight of the emaciated yet swollen body, caused me to wince and draw back.

But that was my last retreat from reality. Later, as I helped Nurse Layng to dress the naked body in the stiff calico shroud, our eyes met across the still figure. 'You'll do,' she said. 'We all have to go through with it.' With quick, capable fingers, she bandaged the sagging jaw and closed the lids over the staring eyes, weighting them down with the customary pennies. The ordeal was over.

When I went into the kitchen to help with the mid-morning lunches, Bridie looked at me. 'So he's gone, the poor unfortunate,' she said. 'God rest his soul. The Mother of God will be looking after him now.'

Almost without realizing it, I found myself murmuring, 'Amen.'

14

One of my most harrowing experiences was being sent to work on Ward 16, popularly known as the Top Floor. A real anomaly, it was divided into four sections, not including the clinical theatre: two separate four-bed wards, each with a balcony for fresh air, for tubercular men and women; a diptheria ward for children; a ward for septic cases; and strangest of all, a maternity and labour ward.

'Abandon hope' should have been written above those TB wards. Even my untrained eye could see that these were terminal cases. The women were young, though the disease had erased all signs of youth. One of them was up and walking around in her dressing gown. She came in from the balcony.

'Just getting a breath of fresh air, Nurse,' she said, 'or what passes for it. I'm from the country, and it doesn't seem very fresh to me.' Then she asked, 'Are you the new nurse?'

'Very new. You must help me, please,' I responded.

I must have sensed her resentment at the enforced idleness, and my comment struck the right note, for her dull eyes brightened and she half-smiled in response, 'I'm going to like you.'

As she spoke, one of the other patients started to speak out and got caught up by a cough that seemed to drag the very heart out of her. I flew out of the room to find the staff nurse. 'The place isn't on fire, is it?' demanded the lady when I found her dressing a leg in the septic ward. 'No,' I said breathlessly, 'but one of the TB women is coughing, and she's spitting blood.'

'Of course she is,' was the scornful reply. 'They all do, sooner or later.' Then she added, 'Give her a dose of linctus, there's a bottle in the duty room.'

I found the bottle and returned to the ward, wondering if the nurse's apparent indifference was a protection against involvement. Back in the ward I found that the girl's fit of coughing was over; she lay exhausted, eyes closed. The girl in the dressing gown said, 'Let me give you a hand with the odd jobs, Nurse. Days I get so bored I could throw myself from that balcony. Lil's my name. Please don't call me Bed 4; we're such a small party here, and we like to keep our names. That's Liz, her with the cough. And that's Violet in the other corner, and Rosie's in the bathroom.'

When I came off duty from that first day on the Top Floor, I ran a bath and soaked in it for a long time. Then I went in search of my three friends and comfort. I had come up against the hard fact that sometimes death can be a friend.

Having found the three in Wharton's room, I let loose my emotions in a spate of words. 'That Top Floor really has got you down,' commented Maxwell dryly, as I came to a full stop, swallowing the lump in my throat that betrayed my unprofessional involvement.

'It was the smells and the sputum mugs and the hopelessness of it all,' I defended. Wharton put a cup of steaming cocoa into my hand. 'Drink it up,' she ordered, 'and you'll feel better.'

The next morning the staff nurse and I had wheeled two of the TB men on to the balcony when she told me, 'You can tidy up here and make up that empty bed for the admission this afternoon. I'm going to do a couple of dressings in the septic ward.' As she walked out of the ward, she snapped out a warning, 'And don't come after me unless Matron or Sister or any other emergency turns up.'

Andy, the boy left in the ward after we wheeled the other two out, muttered, 'Proper old battle-axe, that one.' I pretended not to hear as I hurried away to get linen for the empty bed. When I returned, he was lying on his side, watching the door. His emaciated face was flushed, and he was plucking at his sheet with nervous fingers. 'Nurse, would you ever, would you ever change my bottom sheet while she's out of the way?'

I looked at him in surprise. 'But we changed your sheets yesterday, Andy.' I was puzzled; no-one had told me he was incontinent.

'I know, but . . .' he paused, and the thin face turned an even deeper crimson as he struggled to explain. 'I didn't meant to do it, truly I didn't, Nurse. But I get so bored, so – so desperate.'

Still puzzled, but realizing this was a genuine cry for help, I decided to risk raiding the linen room on my own. When I got back to the ward, weak as he was, Andy had struggled out of the bed and into the chair.

I stripped the bed. This was not incontinence, but there was certainly a stain on the undersheet. His anxious and embarrassed gaze was on me. 'You won't tell the doctor, Nurse?'

'Tell him what, Andy?'

'I'm ashamed to speak of it, Nurse. I didn't ought—' But here a paroxysm of coughing took over and choked him into silence. By the time I had given him a dose of linctus, Sister had appeared, and I had to go in search of Nurse Martin.

That night I sought out Symonds. 'What was he trying to tell me?' I asked, when I had described the whole incident. 'Why should he be ashamed?'

'You've still got a lot of eggshell sticking to you, chick,' she said. We were sitting side by side on her bed. She raised an arm and took down a dictionary that was lying on top of her chest of drawers. She opened it and ran her finger down a column of the 'M' section. 'Here it is,' she said, as she handed me the book, 'your question answered.' Her finger pointing to the enlightening word. 'Read it; you're learning about life as you never knew it.'

I shall always believe that it was the depression caused by my three weeks on the Top Floor that nearly drove me into the potentially explosive emotional outlet offered by an old friend.

Perhaps more women than we realize have someone in their lives whose memory always brings with it the question, 'How could I? I must have been mad.' In my case, it happened this way.

I was coming off duty from the Top Floor and it was my weekend off. A probationer's weekend stretched from 6 p.m. on Saturday to 10 p.m. on Sunday. This brief spell of freedom occurred once a month – not much in terms of the moving hands of the clock, but in terms of appreciation, every minute was worth sixty of those I had never counted in the past.

I rushed to my room, changed, and was picking up my overnight case when there was a knock at the door. 'Gentleman to see you, Nurse, I've put him in the sitting room.' Puzzled and a little excited, I hurried along to the sitting room. And there he was. Hair a bit greyer, but deep-set eyes still alive with the twinkle I had responded to, even as a small girl. He was fun. He had always been fun, a good companion. But he was also danger. I made no excuses; I was no longer a little girl to be mesmerized.

He held out both hands for mine. 'It's been a hell of a long time,' he said. I nodded dumbly, for the old magic was working havoc. He picked up my case.

'I'm going home for the weekend,' I told him.

'I'll take you to the station,' he said. 'We can make plans in the taxi.'

On the short journey to Charing Cross there was not a look or a word to scare me; he was the concerned father-uncle figure. I promised to lunch with him on Monday. I was going on night duty the next week, so the first half of that day would be free.

The pleasure of my weekend at home was overlaid by an instinctive feeling of guilt. I was hiding something from people who loved me. 'Nonsense,' I told myself. 'What can be wrong in going to lunch with an old friend?' But when Nanny brought me breakfast in bed and sat down beside me for one of our tell-it-all talks, I was afraid she would discover my secret assignation.

'Well now,' she said, her wise brown eyes on my face, 'you're going on with it? But you've gone a bit skinny. Still, with this war on that's hardly to be wondered at.' I picked up my knife and fork. 'That's the real thing, Miss Dolly, that's not made with egg powder.'

I took a mouthful of the scrambled egg. 'It's delicious,' I told her while my mind searched for something to talk about.

'What's on your mind?' she asked. I nearly choked: as far as I was concerned, Nanny was psychic. In desperation I gave her a detailed description of life on the Top Floor. This, plus a breakfast eaten to the last crumb, seemed to satisfy her. 'And why not?' I told myself angrily. 'I'm only going out to lunch with an old friend.'

Monday morning; 'Nurse Bishop on night duty' was the posting. And Nurse Bishop going out. I looked at the two or three dresses hanging behind the curtain in my room. The blue silk? I held it up for consideration. Too fussy for lunch, I decided, and took out the grey muslin with green sprigs that would be more suitable. I laid it on the bed.

Twelve o'clock. I hastily dabbed powder on my nose. (A swansdown puff and a box of powder was about the only

112

concession most of us made to make-up.) As I adjusted my hat, a knock came. 'Gentleman to see you, Nurse.'

It didn't look like a restaurant to me, not the kind I was used to, anyway. It was a shabby pub somewhere in the back streets of Soho, certainly not a part of Soho I had ever visited. He was paying off the taxi, and suddenly I felt trapped. He took my arm – the uncle-cum-father touch to give reassurance. 'I've booked a private room,' he said, as we entered the dimly lit saloon bar. Tawdry, my mind registered as I looked around. An oily-looking individual came out from behind the bar.

'Josef will take you upstairs, Monsieur,' he told my companion. Josef was a bent little gnome of a man in a dirty striped waistcoat and baize apron. I began to feel that something was very wrong. There were perhaps half a dozen men seated at the bar, presided over by a flashy-looking woman, who had used all the aids she knew to create the illusion of youth. All these people seemed to be casting furtive glances in our direction.

My skin felt hot and prickly as we followed the gnome up the stairs. At the top of the short flight he opened a door and stood back for us to enter. There was a sort of sly and greedy look in his eyes, and he almost snatched the tip dropped into his grimy hand. 'Will that be all, Monsieur?'

'For the moment, yes.' The door closed. I stood quite still in the middle of the floor. A fly-spotted mirror in a tarnished gilt frame took up one wall of the small square room. There were a couple of red plush and gilt chairs underneath the window. The summer sunshine was struggling to penetrate its soot-stained panes. Beneath the mirror was a red plush couch.

I could no longer evade the obvious. This was no setting for a harmless lunch for two. 'Come, little one,' he said, as I stood like a figure turned to stone. 'I don't have to spell things out for you, do I? I have waited a long time for this. I left you alone when you were beautiful with the bloom of extreme youth; I tried you out later – you must remember.'

I did indeed remember, and the memory made me wince. Then his arms were round me, and his lips were on mine. In a rush of shame and fury I broke loose. I reached the door before he did and stumbled down the stairs. My cheeks flaming and my head held high, I walked through the saloon bar, barely conscious of the knowing glances that followed me out of the swinging doors. But I was only too aware of the comments that

113

started up as I escaped. My self-respect was shattered. As I hurried along the sunlit streets, the thought of that plush couch made me shudder, and I felt like a leper warning society, 'Unclean, unclean.'

But life has to be lived hour by hour. Even the most shattering experience must be absorbed. I was just a cog in a great machine, and I had my part to play in its running. As I walked up the stairs of the Nurses' Home, I once more became a 'less than the dust' probationer nurse, a slave of the lamp lit by Florence Nightingale, not so very long ago. Frankie Mason's father and the plush couch had besmirched a lovely day, but that was all. I had learned another lesson.

Mechanically, I began to undress, hanging the grey muslin dress behind the curtain, folding up every garment. After I had pulled down the blind to shut out the sunshine that mocked the idea of sleep, I crept into bed. But the strange bedtime, plus the shock and emotional turbulence I had just been through, made sleep impossible. Just when I seemed to be dropping off, footsteps in the corridor, the flapping of the blind as a soft breeze came and went, would be enough to rouse me.

I gave up. I got out of bed, stuck my feet into slippers, and took my dressing gown from behind the curtain. I would go up to the flat lead roof. Here there was always shade under one of the great chimney stacks, and little wandering breezes seemed to belong there. Sometimes it resembled the deck of a cruising liner with deck chairs, cushions and scattered hairpins (because it was ideal for hair drying). Sometimes the sour-faced porter swept up cigarette butts as well as hairpins, but he had his good points; he never reported this to Home Sister. Even off-duty smoking was strictly forbidden and Sisters had been known to sniff at suspects' keyholes – or so rumour said.

So much was frowned on and forbidden in those days. Smoking, socializing with the housemen, marriage. If a nurse dared to marry while she was training, well, that was the end of her career. In those days of wartime marriages, there were nurses who would risk their final certificates. We would conspire together to keep her secret. Harder to hide was a case of morning sickness, but somehow we managed that too.

I picked up my pillow and made for the roof. Wharton was there, kneeling on a rug, watching the uncertain flame of a spirit stove. *Black's Medical Dictionary* and *Taylor's Manual of*

Nursing had been propped up round it to act as a wind screen. Symonds was lying back in a deck chair, a lighted cigarette in her hand. 'Welcome to the party. You look a bit off colour, child,' she said brightly, blue eyes assessing me as I squatted on the rug where Maxwell was seated cross-legged, mending one of the black stockings we all wore on duty.

Symonds laid her free hand on my tousled head. She liked to play the mother figure, and we played along with her, spilling out our troubles and asking for advice. But this was one occasion when I held my own counsel; the episode must remain a shameful secret.

So we had our picnic up there on the roof, and when the three went back on duty I returned to bed. And this time I slept.

15

'Seven o'clock, Nurse.'

It was a cruel summons. I had only just dropped off to sleep – or so it seemed. Half-awake, I reached the dining room with little appetite for the kipper that was the twin of one I had eaten for breakfast a few hours earlier. But I was concerned to know where I would be sent and when Night Sister moved along the line to stand beside my chair, I jumped up – a puppet on a string. 'Nurse Bishop, you will go to Ward 3.' Ward 3 was the gynaecological ward. A step up, for the night probationer did some of the treatment, such things as enemas and douches.

University College Hospital clung to the system of meals eaten in the ward kitchen, when possible. The night pro collected the meagre material for these meals: hot buttered toast made up the necessary bulk, but for butter read margarine, and the margarine of those days could certainly not be mistaken for butter.

Breakfast over, I joined the queue of night probationers who were being handed the carrying baskets in which they packed their night's rations. The staff nurses had moved on, swinging their 'Dorothy bags' – small embroidered carryalls with draw-strings, which were fashionable at that time. At last came my turn. Night Sister handed me two rissoles, two bananas, and two small pats of margarine in an enamel container. I put this into my basket, closed the lid, and was set for the night's work.

The night was hot and close, so the swing doors of the ward were open. Lights were out except for the shaded lamp on Sister's desk at the far end of the room. There was a central pillar, and I noted the four cots, one at each corner of the pillar.

I had never had anything to do with babies before. I crept past Sister's desk as she gave the report to the Night Staff. I found a kettle singing on the gas stove in the kitchen and a stone hot-water bottle waiting to be filled. I set down my basket beside the jar on the deal flap which was hinged to the wall, serving as a table. I was filling the jar when the Night Staff walked in.

'Thanks,' she said, in a quiet and gentle voice that complemented her vivacious dark face. As I screwed the top on she added, 'It's for me; I get cold feet sitting at Sister's desk making up dressings for the drums. My name's Dawson, and I hope we team up well. This is your first night duty, isn't it?'

'Yes,' I answered with a nod, adding 'and I don't know what to do.'

'There has to be a first time,' smiled Nurse Dawson. 'I'm not an ogre and I'll sketch things out for you when we've settled up the patients. Actually they're all quiet now, so come into the ward with me.'

We seated ourselves at Sister's desk, and I listened as she briefed me as to my duties – which, it seemed, would keep me on my feet for every minute of every hour throughout the night. The recital finished, Nurse Dawson smiled. 'It sounds worse than it is. Now, you go back to the kitchen and start off by setting the breakfast trays and putting them on the trolley. And I'll do my round of the patients.'

Setting the trays; cleaning bowls, basins and sinks; scrubbing shelves and rubber sheets; polishing the sterilizing drums (Ward 3 had its own small theatre), occupied me till about 11.30. The night seemed to be stretching into infinity when finally I looked at my watch and consulted the list of extra work for night nurses which hung on the kitchen dresser.

As no nurse could ever be seen to be idle, extra was the word for time-fillers. These tasks were varied, but one I came to dread was the sewing of stiff calico shrouds. It gave me sore, pricked fingers, and nightmares resulted from the crude reminder of death, the enemy we so often fought in vain, in those days without antibiotics or other modern aids.

But before turning to extra work, I had to 'borrow' bread from another ward – a common practice that helped to break the monotony of daily routine. 'Try 7,' advised Nurse Dawson. I picked up a plate from the dresser and started off down the backstairs, an open fire escape route that was popular with the night staff when spring and summer nights made the wards stuffy and oppressive.

For a few minutes I hung over the iron rails, looking down

117

into the street below. It was very quiet, and the dark street, like all London streets under the blackout law, seemed to harbour sinister shadows. Sounds seemed sharper in their impact. I heard the footsteps of a patrolling policeman long before he passed the hospital walls. The only other sound was the faint, sporadic rumble of traffic in Gower Street.

I sat for a few minutes on the iron stairway, wondering how my vocation was shaping, when I would get beyond this perpetual scrubbing, dusting and polishing. What was it Symonds had said last week, when I had spilt something of this discouragement into her sympathetic ear? 'Don't panic. We mustn't be put off by the present, it's only a stepping stone to the future. While we polish the taps over the doctors' basins, we can be checking up on our last lecture, readying ourselves for the exams coming up in the autumn.'

She was right of course. Jumping up, I drew in a deep breath of cool air, and continued on my way.

When I returned, I set about preparing Nurse Dawson's meal, heating up a rissole, making toast and tea. Going into the ward to tell her the meal was ready, I found her holding the hand of a goblin-like creature. 'Tiny has a pain in her head and can't sleep,' said Nurse Dawson. I took her other hand and was moved by a sudden wave of compassion.

Tiny was a cretin, six months pregnant. I had heard her story through the hospital grapevine. As Nurse Dawson slipped away into the kitchen, a thin streak of moonlight filtered through the blackout curtains. It revealed the incredible network that made Tiny's face a fantastic mask. Her story was a revelation of perverted sex. This was incest shown up in startling reality. I had read Byron's 'Beatrice Cenci', but it did not have the impact of this sordid bit of prose. As if she read my thoughts, Tiny stared up at me, assessing me as a child does, aware that she held all my attention. Then she held out her arms. 'Tiny tired,' she said.

The finger of moonlight that had pierced the crack in the blackout now picked up the bald patches in the large unwieldy head as she bent forward so that I could hold and comfort her. Nurse Dawson, returning from the kitchen with hot milk and aspirin, found me laying the heavy head on the pillows. Tiny had fallen asleep. I straightened up with a sigh.

'Nurse!'

I looked about me, trying to locate the whisper.

'Nurse, it's me, Mrs 14.'

I tiptoed along to Bed 14.

'Have you got such a thing as a cup of tea, dearie?' came the wheedling tone, as she raised her head from the pillow.

'I'll see,' I replied noncommittally, and went along to the kitchen. Nurse Dawson looked up from *Nash's Magazine*, which was propped against the teapot. She smiled.

'Mrs 14, I suppose. I'm afraid I've spoiled her. She always asks for tea at this time. I suspect she lies awake waiting for it.' She removed the magazine and, lifting the lid, looked into the teapot. 'Hand me a mug, please, Nurse.'

I returned to the ward with the mugful of tea. Mrs 14 received it with a sigh of satisfaction. 'Thanks ever so, dearie. Nurse Johnson, she useter get me out a biscuit from me locker.' Nurse Johnson was the night pro I had replaced; I felt like sticking pins into this do-gooder. Mrs 14 was speaking again: 'And if you wouldn't mind getting out me sugar as well, it's somewhere between me corsets and me boots – a small round tin.' As I searched in the dark, my fingers made direct contact with a pot of butter, but finally I got hold of the tin of sugar and the biscuits.

Mrs 14 sat up, her florid face creased into a smile. 'Thanks ever so, dearie. And Nurse Johnson, she useter shake up me pillows, so she did.' I stuck a few more pins into Nurse Johnson's image as I meekly obeyed. I was then dismissed with the words, 'I don't think I'll have to trouble you again, Nurse.' You'd better not, was my unspoken thought, checked when I remembered that patience was part of a nurse's mission.

Nurse Dawson came into the ward. 'Now you go get your meal,' she said. This I did, warming up my rissole without much enthusiasm, trying to ignore the cockroaches that were scurrying up and down the walls, one or two dropping on to the white tablecloth.

And now it was 1 a.m., the dawn of a new day. Night Sister had done her first round, and the housemen had also come and gone. The ward was quiet, and an almost painful drowsiness was overtaking me. I decided to start cutting the bread for breakfast, which proved an agonizing task. Several times I found myself nodding and then jerking myself back to the job at hand. Night Sister making her second round and babies crying were almost welcome stimulation.

When dawn broke, all was quiet once more, and staff and pro sat on the back stairs sipping mugs of tea, getting to know each other as Gower Street and the Euston Road were wakened into life by the heavy lorries roaring their way to Covent Garden and the other city markets.

Just before 4 a.m. the new day's work began. 'It seems like cruelty,' I said, as we collected the douche cans and bedpans from the sink room. 'Some of them have only just dropped off to sleep.'

'It can't be helped,' was the reply. 'As it is, we shall barely have finished before the day staff come on.'

And she was right. Breakfasts were supposed to be taken round at 6 o'clock, but it was already ten minutes past when I wheeled the metal trolley into the ward with its first load of trays. The patients in this ward were treated to individual teapots, each marked with a small square of sticking plaster on which was pencilled the number of a bed. Getting to know the teapots was of first importance, a task not helped by the near illegibility of some of the plasters. Midway on my round, a tray took a jolt and slithered on to the floor. My morale was shattered. A few moments of panic were relieved by Nurse Dawson's help, and as I handed out the last tray, I felt a great load lifted from my wilting back.

The night's work not yet finished, I collected the trays. The patients' friends sometimes brought eggs to supplement the bread and margarine that was standard fare, and now I was told, 'You boiled my eggs just right, Nurse.' Two or three patients praised my tea-making, and the words, 'That Nurse Johnson couldn't boil an egg nor make a cup of tea fit for a Christian to drink', were music to my ears – at least some did not find that do-gooder perfect.

When I came off duty at 7 a.m., hashed mutton and maize pudding seemed quite acceptable to one now translated into the topsy-turvy world of night duty.

16

Finished with night duty in Ward 3, I was sent to Casualty, which was ruled by the oldest sister in the hospital.

The layout of Casualty was daunting in itself: the great waiting room, with its scrubbed wooden benches; the dingy little aseptic cubicles, like prison cells; the small operating theatre. Then there was the all-pervading legend that was Sister Jane. But those who passed through Sister Jane's hands and were approved – however grudgingly – would be assured of their final certificate.

That first morning, while I was screwing up my courage to find someone to tell me where to go and what to do, I felt like a traveller lost in a vast desert. Suddenly, a short dumpy figure appeared from nowhere. The dark blue of her uniform proclaimed her rank; a commanding air of dignity that was worthy of Queen Victoria told me it was the dreaded Sister Jane, ruler of this underworld.

'Hmm,' she said curtly, 'so you're what Matron has sent me.' The quick eyes behind steel-rimmed glasses looked searchingly over me. 'Your cap's on crooked; put it straight.'

I put a shaking hand up to obey.

'You look a big gazy; what's your name?'

I stammered out my name.

'Speak up, woman, I won't eat you.'

I was not so sure of that.

'Bishop, Nurse Bishop.'

'Well, Nurse, you'll have work to do here. You'll kindly remember that you are not just an ornament.' Then, after a terrifying pause, and after once more looking me up and down and, I felt sure, through and through, she suddenly barked, 'Can you scrub?'

The question was so totally unexpected, that I opened my mouth to speak and no words emerged. Then, as speech returned, I blurted out, 'I – I think so, Sister.'

'You think, do you? You ought to know by this time. Can you scrub? Yes or no?'

Had I known my interrogator better, I might have said no. Instead, I took a chance and said, 'Yes, Sister. Where shall I find soap, please, Sister?'

'Soap? Soap? Do you suppose I carry round soap and brushes for my probationers? Remember this: if you ever again forget that I am the Sister here, off you go to the Matron.'

The last words were spoken over her shoulder as she trotted away. I had started to follow her when, suddenly, she swivelled round and we nearly collided.

'Where do you think you're going, Nurse?' The sharp eyes glared at me. 'I won't have you chasing after me like this. It's a waste of time. And nothing is to be wasted here, not time, nor breath, nor even words – nothing at all.' Once more she trotted away, eyes on the ground.

Baffled, I walked in the opposite direction. To my relief, I found a staff nurse washing down some shelves in the theatre.

'So you're the new pro – heaven help you. But one word of advice, the more scared you look, the more she'll run you around. She barks and snaps, but there's a lot of good behind that grouchy front.'

I nodded, not convinced. 'I was told to scrub,' I said nervously, 'but what am I to scrub?'

'Come and take your cuffs off in the duty room,' I was told, 'and I'll see what I can do.'

Finally, I was found a table to scrub at the far end of the waiting room, given the soap and a brush, and shown where to get a bowl and where to fill it with hot water. I set to work, feeling the tension leaving me as I dipped my brush in the suds. I could not go wrong here, I thought. Then Sister Jane reappeared.

'What are you doing, Nurse? Who told you to scrub that table? Do you call that scrubbing?'

'I thought—' I stammered before I was interrupted.

'You thought, did you? I am the one who does the thinking here. You carry out my orders.' She snatched the brush from me, rolled up her sleeves, and started to scrub with relentless vigour. Then, wiping the table clean of suds, she turned to me. '*That* is scrubbing; up and down, following the grain of wood. Whatever else I do – or do not do – I train my nurses to scrub.

Don't stand there gaping, put away these things and be quick about it. Then follow me.'

After half an hour, I was back where I had started, in the waiting room. It was beginning to fill up with the flotsam and jetsam of the streets around the hospital. I had toured what seemed like miles of boxed-in cubicles, trying to take in Sister Jane's running commentary. Now I stood clutching a little black book of written instructions, which I found more confusing than helpful.

In Casualty, I was a sort of handmaiden to the various specialists – the eye specialist; the ear, nose and throat consultant; the skin specialist. I set out their tables with the instruments and other paraphernalia, and woe betide me if I put one item in the wrong place. Mercifully, I had something of a photographic memory. I ushered in their patients, having checked the cards they held in grubby hands. I chaperoned the female patients. Soon I began to get a measure of entertainment out of this unique centre of activity.

I marvelled at Sister Jane's masterly shepherding of these rather gormless specimens of humanity:

'Ma'am, don't argue with me – go and sit over there.'

'My good man, don't contradict. You've come here for advice, and I'm here to see that you get it.'

'This is not a teashop, Ma'am. Kindly take the bun away from your little boy – who may also wipe his nose.'

And they obeyed the sharp, barking voice and sat on the benches, deflated, empty of all protest. They knew, for all her odd ways and sharp tongue, that Sister Jane of Casualty was their friend.

I also became aware of that core of kindness. On one occasion, when I went to relay a message from the staff nurse and I had one of my rare headaches, she looked me up and down. 'What you need is a breath of fresh air,' she said. 'Go to Mudie's, if you know where that is, and change my books. No need to dawdle, I shall expect you back in half an hour.'

As far as anyone could settle down in Casualty, I did. I managed to keep out of the way of Sister's domination, and I certainly learned to scrub. In fact, it seemed to me I had become a general dogsbody for Sister and her staff. One of my jobs was boiling up the various instruments and laying them out again on their respective sterilizers. You lit a gas ring under the enamel sterilizer, and always in the back of your mind was the nightmare of burning it out.

I was sewing a shroud one mid-November morning and watching the clock as instruments bubbled and boiled over the blue flame of the gas ring. I was a clumsy seamstress at best, and the stiff calico meant sore pricked fingers. But I was no longer depressed by the gruesome thoughts that the shrouds had previously brought. At least here, I thought, people died in their beds, looked after, their passing eased in every possible way. Whereas, across the Channel . . . I shivered, biting off the thread with my teeth as I finished the hem.

'Nurse, you have, or should have, a pair of scissors in your pocket.'

The neat little figure in blue glared at me through the open door and, without another word, passed on. I looked at the clock. Two minutes to go before I turned off the gas. I got up and started to fold my work. Then I looked round, conscious that someone else was standing in the doorway.

I was grabbed by a stocky figure in khaki. Cuthbert!

'Come on girl! Forty-eight hours leave. Let's find that Sister and fix things up.'

'I can't,' I wailed. 'Sister Jane would never—'

'Leave her to me,' he interrupted. 'Just tell me where to find her.'

'She's everywhere,' I moaned, 'and anywhere.'

'Defeatist!' He grinned and walked away.

I whirled into the feverish activity of tidying up, hurrying away to retrieve a scrubbing dish left in one of my cubicles. Returning to the sterilizing room, I was greeted by acrid smoke. Hope died within me. The sterilizer had burned dry. I must have turned off the gas, because the sinister crackling sound ceased, but my mind felt numb and overwhelmed. I stood as if rooted to the floor as all the implications of the disaster rushed in on me.

After a while – it could have been minutes or hours – I heard voices. Cuthbert had found her, and there they were, talking as equals. But I had ruined everything! Hot tears began to roll down my cheeks.

'Nurse Bishop,' barked the little figure in blue, 'you will now go off duty and will report to me in my office tomorrow morning at 10 a.m.'

It was unbelievable – as though a burned-out sterilizer was of no consequence. I didn't know what to say.

'Thank you, Sister,' said Cuthbert quietly, taking his cue. 'My fault. It was too sudden and upsetting.'

They shook hands. A salute. As we walked away together, I felt like someone who had witnessed a miracle.

'They don't come in duplicate,' was my brother's cryptic remark.

Two weeks later I left Casualty and the legend that was Sister Jane, with only a burned-out sterilizer to blot my copybook, or so I hoped.

17

My first Christmas in hospital. I think I learned the full meaning of that Christian feast when I woke up on Christmas Eve and realized with surprise that I was not homesick.

I was back in Ward 8, and for once the status barriers were all down: Sisters, staff nurses and probationers were all united in the democracy of loving and giving. That evening, as we sat in the ward kitchen making last-minute paperchains, wrapping up presents for our patients, Sister came in with a bottle of sherry. 'From Matron,' she told us, smiling as she set it down on the table. 'So if Nurse Brown will get a corkscrew and some glasses, we'll celebrate.'

But even as she spoke the Junior Staff, who had been left in charge of the ward, came hurrying in.

'It's Johnnie in Bed 12, Sister,' she said, her round pink face troubled and concerned. 'He's sobbing away and saying "I don't want to die, Sister. Tell Sister I don't want to die." I can do nothing with him,' she finished, 'and it's upsetting the other patients.'

Sister, who had just sat down beside me, got up. 'I'll give him an injection,' she said, adding, 'You get the dressing trolley and Nurse Bishop can come with me and put screens round his bed.'

My heart gave a great thump, and then seemed to stop still. Like a mechanical figure I followed Sister into the ward. There were uneasy turnings and whispers as we walked between the two rows of beds. The lamp on Sister's desk shed a pool of light on the polished parquet floor and there was a red-shaded light over Bed 12.

Ten-year-old Johnnie had cancer – sarcoma of the hip. He had been admitted that morning to one of the empty beds in Ward 8 because the Children's Ward was full. Mr Williams, our senior consultant surgeon, had brought along his students to see him that afternoon.

We knew him as 'the butcher', a name given to him by the theatre nurses who suffered from his forthright speech, which they resented as the crack of the ringmaster's whip. He was a brilliant surgeon, but no psychiatrist; he discussed the patients, and lectured his students at the bedside as if they were inanimate teaching models. His parting words as he walked away from Johnnie's bed were all too plain, and the little cockney boy had missed nothing of their meaning.

While I manoeuvred the heavy wooden screens round Johnnie's bed, Sister bent over him with soothing words, baring the skinny little arm for the injection. His big dark eyes were wet with tears which trickled down his pale thin face. All the while, he kept moaning, 'Sister I don't want to die.' My own eyes filled with tears, but by a supreme effort of will I checked the overflow – emotional involvement could be no part of a nurse's training.

After Sister had given Johnnie the injection, Nurse Layng wheeled away the trolley. 'Sit here with him, Nurse,' Sister told me. 'The injection should take effect shortly. Tell him a story – it helps.'

I sat down beside his bed and took one of the hot little hands in mine. 'Tell him a story.' The words echoed in my mind, shocked into emptiness. Then suddenly, the story of Jethro's daughter flashed into my thoughts.

'Johnnie,' I said softly, turning towards him, 'sometimes doctors can be mistaken. I'll tell you about a little girl who was so ill that the doctors told her father and mother, "There is nothing more we can do; she will die."' I paused, noting the flicker of interest in the dark eyes. Then I continued, drawing on pictures I remembered from a child's book of Bible stories which my mother used to read to us long ago. The absorbed interest of my listener as he identified himself with Jethro's little daughter was palpable.

'She is not dead but sleepeth.' And then I added – although it felt as if it was someone else who spoke – 'So you see, Johnnie, that doctors can be wrong.'

'And she had no more pain, Nurse?'

'No more pain, Johnnie.'

His eyes closed and he slept.

As I got up to report to Sister, Nurse Layng, sitting at Sister's desk, whispered as I passed by, 'Well done, Nurse.' But suddenly I felt drained of all sensation – like a child lost in a black and frightening forest.

'May God forgive me,' I said to someone I used to know when answers were written in black and white. But my healthy body reasserted a sense of balance and I slept soundly that night, though tears dried on my face.

As I walked into Ward 8 on Christmas morning, I looked at Bed 12. It was empty. Nurse Layng read my thoughts.

'He was admitted to 5 late last night. It's better for him and better for us . . .' At least in the Children's Ward he would not be so isolated.

That day in Ward 8, I found a Christmas spirit such as I had never known in the self-contained world of family celebration. The great tree at the end of the ward was alight with candles and hung with parcels for our patients, collected by Sister throughout the year. Later, our senior consultant physician, Dr Bolton, would dress up as Santa to take these gifts from the tree, and other consultants and their wives would arrive for tea and carols. Even a jovial Mr Williams had his assigned role – to carve the turkey for the patients' dinner.

Housemen popped in and out dressed up for clowning, whilst we nurses went from ward to ward singing carols. We had practised in the evenings when we came off duty; standing round the old scratched piano in the nurses' sitting room with Home Sister often our conductor.

And Matron – the mother figure – making a visit to every ward; admiring, not censuring. She knew the big vases of flowers and the holly and mistletoe came from a grateful Covent Garden Market, fetched by her Sisters and their senior staffs in the small hours of Christmas Eve. The porters and the stallholders of that market knew an angel in disguise, long blue cloaks and elastic-sided boots replacing the traditional wings.

18

'Nurse Bishop to Ward 7.' I was on the move again.

Ward 7 was Women's Medical. It seemed a haven of peace after the two hectic and uneasy months I had spent in Casualty. That is, until McSweeney.

'So you are the junior pro here,' she remarked as we removed our cuffs in the kitchen and pulled on our sleeves. She sounded as if my status were a slur on the ward. 'Well, this is a busy place,' she continued, 'so don't come running to ask me this and that.'

'I've been here a week,' I told her coldly, 'so don't worry, I won't.'

I looked at her unsmiling face. Why did she have such a chip on her shoulder? And why did she have to pick on me? I went into the sink room and filled one of the enamel basins with water.

As I walked towards the patient in Bed 15, she smiled – a wispy little woman with hair dyed a bright gold that only emphasized the pallor of her face. A so-called pernicious anaemia case, she managed to keep cheerful on a diet of nearly raw liver. My face must have given away my feelings about drawing McSweeney as a colleague for Mrs 15 asked, 'Bad news, Nurse?'

I managed a smile. 'In a way, yes,' I replied. 'But nothing I can't cope with.' At that moment McSweeney appeared.

'Gawd 'elp us,' muttered my patient. 'She was 'ere on nights for a week temporary – and were we glad to see the back of 'er.'

For some reason this comment about my senior colleague bothered me. I felt sorry for McSweeney and the dislike and resentment she aroused. Also, there was such a thing as professional loyalty, I reminded myself. 'It's just her manner,' I assured Mrs 15, as I bent down to get her soap and flannel from the locker. 'It's . . . well, she's all right, really.'

'Sez you,' was the dry comment.

A few days later I was giving Mrs 15 a blanket bath, a process that was rather like unwrapping a parcel. Having arranged a rubber sheet and blanket under your patient, you then swathed the protesting body in another blanket, after the deft removal of nightshirt or nightgown. Then, limb by limb, you unwrapped the parcel, washing each exposed bit and then rewrapping it. It was quite a performance. In the midst of the procedure, we heard a commotion at the far end of the ward. I poked my head round the screens. 'An emergency,' I told Mrs 15, as I dried the last bit of her skinny little body. 'Now,' I added, 'turn over, I want to rub your back with spirit.'

'Well it won't do no good, but it won't do no 'arm neither I suppose,' commented the patient, as she rolled on to her side.

'If I didn't rub your back, you'd get bedsores,' came my best professional manner.

Just before 6 o'clock that evening, McSweeney rushed into the kitchen, where I was filling the big kettle at the sink, her thin face scarlet with annoyance. She dumped two stone jars on the table. 'Nurse Lamb knows I've got the evening off,' she spluttered. 'It's pure spite telling me to refill these jars before I go off.'

An impulse from deep down in my conscious self moved me to say, 'Leave it to me. I'll fill them for you as soon as this kettle boils.' With a sort of choking grunt I took for thanks, she rushed back into the ward. When the kettle came to the boil, I emptied the jars, refilled them, and left them on the table. I little knew it was one of those trivial acts that sometimes have the repercussions of a sledgehammer.

The next morning, as we walked up the ward, Mrs 15 beckoned to me. 'Nurse,' she whispered, her pale blue eyes alight with excitement, 'there's a proper fuss going on over there,' and she jerked her thumb to indicate the group of figures just outside the screened bed opposite. 'And that there McSweeney's in it,' she added with relish.

It was none of my business. The fuss concerned McSweeney's patient in a diabetic coma, the emergency that had occurred the day before as I was giving Mrs 15 her bath. I walked into the kitchen to take off my cuffs and put on my sleeves. 'There's trouble out there in the ward, and that McSweeney's in it,' said the ward maid, sipping a cup of tea to buoy her up for polishing the ward floor.

130

Screens, a consultation, and McSweeney caught up in it. Extra work for me. 'I must get a move on,' I said, and went into the sink room to collect a bowl of hot water. As I put out my hand to turn the tap, an arm reached and grabbed me.

McSweeney, her face white and contorted, blurted out, 'Help – you've got to help. The coma patient has been burned by a jar. You filled them, but I put them in her bed, remember?' She shook my arm in desperation. 'Well I've told Sister you put them in.' She was almost incoherent in her rushing spate of words. 'Well I've told Sister you put them in,' she repeated. 'Do you understand?' I just stood there, stiff and speechless. 'You'll be blamed. I said you did it for me because I was going off duty. Mother of God! Do you understand?

'You have everything,' and her voice was shaking and hoarse. 'Love, security, happiness, and I have nothing. Nothing,' she repeated bitterly. 'Nobody here likes me. They'd sack me for a thing like this. And no-one would notice. But they all like you. You're safe. Will you take the blame for this? You don't like me any more than I like you, but for pity's sake, help me.'

'Very well, McSweeney – but keep out of my sight as much as you can.'

I shook her off. A sort of despair seized me as I surrendered to the thought of a dark future. Within minutes the inevitable happened – confrontation with irate authority. Sister McDougal summoned me. She led me into the linen room, out of the sight and hearing of curious eyes and ears.

'Nurse, I'm bitterly disappointed in ye.' When she was worried or upset, Sister reverted to the lilting of her native land. 'To burn an unconscious patient with a hot jar,' she continued, 'why it's criminally careless. And mark you, we don't know where it will end. I've known cases brought to court before this. And ye know what that would mean, do ye not?'

I knew all right. In all probability it would mean disgrace and dismissal. 'Yes, Sister,' I replied, in a toneless whisper. And all to save McSweeney's skin, I told myself. And there was no-one in whom I could confide; I was utterly and bleakly alone.

'I'll not report ye to Matron unless I have to,' went on the sad, kind voice. 'From what I've seen of your work for the wee while you've been in my ward I've found you conscientious and capable. We all make mistakes sometimes, and as a rule we have to pay for them. In this case, I'm sure you've learned your

131

lesson, and I will do my best to shield ye.'

'Thank you, Sister.' There were tears in my eyes that had to be checked before they spilled over. I must go back into the ward, but my whole being cried out for a deep, dark hole in which to hide. Perhaps it was routine that took hold of me and kept me outwardly calm through that seemingly endless day.

'What's the matter with you, chick?' demanded Symonds when I went to her room that night. The strain of that day must have left its mark on me. My head throbbed, and my eyes were red-rimmed from the tears I had let fall unchecked when I came off duty. Now the storm was over, and I was looking for comfort in friendship.

'I'm getting a cold,' I said – which was partly true.

Symonds got up from her bed, which was strewn with notes and text books. 'I'll soon settle that,' she said. 'Sit here on the bed.' She took a coat from behind her curtained alcove and flung it round my shoulders. 'I'm going to rout out some aspirin and hot milk from the other two – I know Wharton brought milk over from the ward.' Thankfully, I let myself be taken over.

But it was, indeed, the start of a cold which defied hot milk and aspirin. I felt the misery I looked when 'Five past six, Nurse', woke me from troubled dreams the next morning. I followed the others into the ward with lagging footsteps. McSweeney, I noted, also looked as though she'd had a sleepless night – as well she might. There were dark rings under her eyes and a grim twist to her thin lips. She walked into the ward a few paces ahead of me. Suddenly she dropped behind and hissed in my ear, 'Look, the bed's empty – we're saved.'

Callous? In a way, I suppose it was. But I own that as I realized the import of her words, a flood of relief swept away the impotent misery and anger that had burned in me for twenty-four hours. It was like waking up in sunshine after being smothered in the darkness of a nightmare. I felt I could face up to anything, even the daily irritant that was McSweeney, and smile.

But the story that an unconscious patient, now dead, had been burned by a hot jar had got around and had to be lived down. My tongue was tied. My friends defended and excused me – and this hurt most of all.

132

Two days later, a reminder of the personal tragedies that were now worldwide jolted back my sense of proportion. At 10 o'clock I had left the ward for the morning tea break. I swallowed a cup of tea and ate a slice of bread and jam, afraid of a pitying glance or a head turned in my direction. On my way back to the ward I met Dagge rushing to her room and sobbing as if her heart would break. In her hand was an open telegram. A brother? Her fiancé perhaps? Killed somewhere in France. I thought of my own three brothers. The darkness and tragedy of war seemed to choke me, as its bloody consequences were rammed home by the sight of the stricken girl.

'Oh, Dagge,' I said, as she rushed past, 'I'm so sorry.' Inadequate words, but I doubt if she heard them. I walked on, reproaching my hypersensitive self. All that fuss about a hot-water jar that caused minor burns, for which I was not even responsible – when I had just seen someone who'd had a vital part of her happiness wrenched from her.

Once more I absorbed myself in the trivia and the sad little dreams of Ward 7. But not all sad. Some had a touch of comedy even.

Our remedies for the common ills of insomnia and consti-pation were not sugar-coated in those days. Though usually effective, they were often revolting. Paraldehyde, prescribed for insomnia, smelled like a compound of everything out of the farmyard. 'Let me hold your nose, dear,' was our usual approach to a patient ordered a dose – a soothing fiction, as they knew and we knew. But there was one old crone who wasn't buying that bit of eyewash.

She was admitted to the ward late one afternoon. She objected to everything in lurid and uncompromising language. And when the fine-tooth comb of the junior staff made its findings, her language spluttered into wild obscenity. Even when she was finally clean and tucked into bed, she looked like the Witch of Endor, with her wisps of grey hair and her malevolent black eyes casting death-ray looks at anyone who approached her bed.

Just before I went off duty that evening, I was deputed to give her a dose of paraldehyde. I should have been on my guard, I suppose, but she seemed quiet, as if the previous violence had drained out of her. A sullen, brooding look was on her face.

'What's that?' she demanded, in a suspicious voice.

'Something to make you sleep,' and I held out the medicine glass as I spoke.

'To hell with you and your filthy muck!' and she took the glass in her claw-like hand and flung it back at me.

If a policeman's life is not a happy one, neither is a probationer nurse's at moments such as this. I rushed up to my room, rinsed out my dress and apron and rammed them into the dirty linen basket. Then I decided to skip supper and soak in a hot bath.

But I liked working in Ward 7. I liked Sister McDougall, and I liked nursing women. I found it less inhibiting than nursing men. In a men's ward, there was always the awkward moment, the embarrassment of sex. I was a bit of Victoriana, and my life had been even more sheltered than most. Symonds once told me, 'A dose of school life would have made things easier for you, child.' She was probably right.

There is one dramatic little incident that bobs about in my memory like a cork in a quiet pond. It seems to me that it represents a whole era of different thinking, different priorities.

I had been loaned to the Children's Ward for a couple of days, in between transfer from night to day duty. On my second day, I was sent to the operating theatre with a baby. Mr Shattock, Surgical Registrar, was to operate.

As I laid the infant down on the trolley in the anaesthetic room, he said, out of the blue, 'Has this child been baptized, Nurse?'

I was taken aback. 'I – I don't know, Sir,' I stammered.

'Go on back to the ward and ask,' he ordered. He stood, a godlike figure in white cap and overall, the pitiless sight of the theatre behind him. 'If he has not been baptized,' he instructed, 'get the mother's permission, and I will baptize him myself.'

What surgeon in this day and age would trouble about the immortal soul of a little scrap of humanity from a London slum? That baptism over a theatre scrubbing-up basin is a recurring picture for me, an unsinkable cork.

19

All through my youth I had been prey to the common cold. But old Nanny had always been at the ready with remedies, hot drinks, and orders for bed, if she thought it necessary, so that after a short spell of runny nose and sore throat the enemy was always well and truly routed.

For a probationer nurse to go sick with a mere cold, though, was unthinkable. When one morning I woke up to the familiar symptoms, the 'five past six' call to duty was a challenge I dared not ignore. I just added a gargle to my sketchy routine of washing and trotted off. But the enemy marched on relentlessly.

'Lor, Nurse, you looks a proper misery,' from one of the patients in Ward 7.

Lozenges were pressed into my hand from well-wishers, and I coughed, sneezed, and battled my way through the day's work. When at last I was finished, I skipped supper and hurried up to my room, flinging myself down on the bed. My body was hot and restless, my face flushed with fever, and my head throbbed with pain.

That was how the other three found me when they came off duty. There was a flurry of consternation, the filling of hot-water bottles, a hot drink, aspirin, and finally, as I laid my throbbing head on the gurgling bag, Symonds went off to find Home Sister.

She came, put a thermometer under my arm, laid her thin, skeletal hand on my wrist, and transferred me to the Old Home, where the elderly radiators generated comforting warmth. There drops were put in my ears, and Night Sister looked in on me when she did her rounds. The final diagnosis? Middle-ear abscess.

Matron and the Resident Medical Officer were at my bedside, debating whether to operate or to wait. I couldn't have cared less either way. When suddenly the abscess discharged its septic menace I was left with a perforated eardrum. For a few days, people floated in and out of my room and I scarcely noticed. I was in my own private heaven of peace. Then, one day, the RMO looked down at me and there was a distinct twinkle in his eye.

'A week of convalescence, Sister,' he said.

Sister looked dubious. The RMO was known (and loved) for his battles with Matron on the subject of sick leave.

I felt tense with a longing for escape – for home, for Nanny, fussing and babying. When I got my week I needed every day of it. But dropping out even for a short while made return to the strict routine of my new life an ordeal, and I found myself shrinking from the very thought. But the three were there handing out cups of tea, telling me they had missed me – their faces warm with welcome. I belonged after all. Once more back in my narrow bed, I slept a dreamless sleep, and the morning call of 'five past six, Nurse' held no terrors for me.

My first morning back, I was sent to work in the Diphtheria Ward for children. There were only a dozen or so patients, all convalescent. They had been caught in time and immunized with the vaccine that was beginning to make its value felt. Nevertheless, the Top Floor certainly played a large part in presenting the darker side of life to me. I had known so little of it that I was probably particularly sensitive to absorbing impressions.

The tragedy of little Lucy May has remained undimmed by time. One morning, coming back to the ward after the ten o'clock tea break, I found Sister and the Staff Nurse lifting a struggling, gasping little figure on to the operating table in a small room off the main ward kept ready for emergencies.

Every second counted as she struggled for breath and the deadly membrane began to strangle and choke its victim to death.

The students stampeded into the small room, headed by a young houseman. Sister bent over the golden head and laid the small white neck down on the sandbags, holding it there with firm strong hands. Tracheotomy: the quick slit with a scalpel that could mean life – or death. The jugular vein, so near the vital area.

'Dear Lord, let him miss it,' I breathed.

The houseman lifted the scalpel from the little tray on the

136

trolley. I saw his hand shake; his face was set and tense. I shut my eyes and time froze into eternity.

'God!'

The stricken exclamation jerked me back into the present, where Lucy May's life was pouring away in a dark red stream. The shaking hand put back the scalpel. The white-faced houseman left with his following of students, their grim lesson learned, a shattered, silent huddle.

My eyes filled with tears. He now had to tell the parents, the elderly couple Sister had shut in her office. Tell them that Lucy May would no longer dance like a sunbeam through their drab lives.

20

That autumn, on top of work on the wards, we had to cope with lectures from the honoraries, with Jimmy the Skeleton and the China Lady. Symonds, the ex-school teacher, was invaluable. Night after night she marshalled our facts, sorted out our problems. *Black's Medical Dictionary* and *Taylor's Manual of Nursing* ruled our spare moments. When I relaxed in a hot bath, I propped one of them up in front of me, and soaked my mind as well as my body.

'Don't worry, they need all of us. Yes, even McSweeney,' said Symonds, giving me a sidelong glance. She was giving the three of us a pep talk the night before the written exam. 'They're desperate for nurses; they won't fail any of us.' Brave words, and probably near the truth, but that didn't prevent me from shaking when I sat down, pen in hand, to answer the printed questions.

The viva voce the next day was even more of an ordeal. One by one, in our immaculate starched whiteness, we were ushered into the torture chamber by Home Sister. Those who came out were met with a barrage of whispers of 'How did it go?' When my turn came, I marched in like a soldier going into battle, and found myself confronted by a seated god, an honorary in striped trousers and frock coat. Beside this intimidating vision sat the China Lady, shameless in her exposure of the *intime*.

Something like a cynical half-smile, outlined by a drooping moustache, greeted me. 'Sit down, Nurse. Take a good look at this model. Then tell me what you know about the liver.' At that moment I was looking at a formless, nebulous world. A true answer would have been 'Nothing'. But I managed to pull myself together and bring the scene before me into focus. I took a deep breath and stammered out a few facts that I hoped might prove relevant.

'Hmm, yes, and this hepatic duct of which you speak, could you point it out to me if you were to remove the liver from this figure?' With shaking fingers I put out my hand, and the cynical half-smile returned as I nearly unhooked the pancreas. I drew back just in time. 'Hmm, yes,' he murmured, 'second thoughts are sometimes best.' Finally I was dismissed with a smile that appeared to be fatherly and encouraging. 'Thank you, Nurse; that will be all.'

The Surgical Registrar, sitting across the room with Jimmy the Skeleton as his companion, greeted me with a friendly grin. I knew him as a friend because Home Sister called him in when any of us needed medical attention. If I seemed to be floundering, he met me more than halfway. Indeed, he seemed to answer many of the questions himself.

Symonds was right. They couldn't afford to lose us. When the list came out, a few days later, she smiled as we walked away from the board where it was posted, and tucked her arm into mine. 'What did I tell you? It really was a bit of a farce. We've all passed.'

One memorable day not long after, I found a long brown paper parcel laid out on my bed. My strings and stripes – the material for the new uniform that showed our step up to junior staff nurse. The stripes referred to the new blue and white material whilst the 'strings' were long strips of muslin which we knotted on top of our heads and tied in a bow under our chins, although we still wore the 'Sister Dora' caps on our heads. Most important of all, this promotion meant we would be transferred to the Old Nurses Home, with its gurgling radiators and its communal gas rings. I could hardly wait.

My first test in my new role was in Ward 15, Men's Surgical. Cheerfulness was the keynote here. People came in, were operated on, and, in most cases, went home having got rid of whatever troubled them. If death came, it was not the long-drawn-out agony we had to cope with in the medical wards, where elderly terminal cases were common.

Another thing that lightened the atmosphere of Ward 15, was that the majority of patients came from comfortable homes, and that implied some sort of education. Ward 8 had been dominated by poverty and ignorance, generated in the slums that lay so close to our front gates. Doctors could cost money, and who could tell what they might do to you once they persuaded you to go into a hospital?

The Sister in Ward 15 was a gentle, caring person. And

shrewd. Nothing escaped those X-ray eyes behind steel-rimmed glasses. Often, she was the one the consultants themselves consulted. Her feet had grown flat in the service of her fellow creatures, but she sailed gallantly up and down the ward in her elastic-sided boots, and never counted the cost of an extra journey.

Sister's pets were put into a corner bed and given protective screens, as well as surreptitious favours such as a china cup and saucer for tea instead of a mug. I remember a certain appendectomy case who caused a tactful reshuffle of beds. He was a lanky young curate, whose slim, too-white hands helped out his hesitant speech in nervous gesticulation. When we saw his mother, we realized the wherefore of the nervous gestures – he was a bad case of 'Mummy's boy'. And when Sister saw his collar, he became Sister's pet – for she was an ardent churchgoer.

His mother haunted us; not actually demanding special treatment for her son, but taking it for granted. Dressed in black, wearing a shabby felt hat with faded pansies as decoration, she would pop up at all sorts of impossible times. She would open the ward doors a crack, peep in, and beckon any nurse who happened to catch her eye. Always some excuse – a bunch of flowers for Sister, a titbit for her boy – anything so that she could look in on her son. He, meanwhile, was watching every movement of the senior pro, whose curves had much to offer a young man's fancy.

The day before he was to have his operation, Sister and I were alone in the ward – a quiet interlude. I was taking down the particulars of a new admittance when Sister came up to tell me she was going out to check the linen room. Sister had hardly disappeared when the ward door opened a few inches. 'Nurse?' There she was, flowers in hand.

I told the new patient to undress and get in bed, and I came out from behind the screens and hurried to prevent any further advance by Mrs Dyer. She thrust the flowers into my hand. I manoeuvred us outside and gently closed the ward door. She produced a brown paper parcel. 'Bedsocks, Nurse. His poor feet get so cold.' She pulled out a handkerchief and wiped her eyes. 'Tomorrow, Nurse – I can't bear to think of tomorrow.'

'Mrs Dyer,' I said, 'come back in an hour. I am alone in the ward, and I must go back.'

'But did he enjoy his fish rissole for breakfast?' she continued. I turned away, combining a noncommittal nod with a smile and beating a cowardly retreat, conscious that the rissole had been left forgotten on the kitchen shelf.

Anaesthesia in those days had some odd after effects. Inhibitions sometimes floated away on clouds of ether. The Reverend John Dyer came out of the anaesthetic the next day using language that was never heard in a pulpit. I was giving treatment to a cheeky young cockney boy in the next bed. 'Gorblimey! Shocking, Nurse. 'Im a reverend, and Sister settin' there alongside of 'im.'

I remember a randy old QC who came into the ward after he had been knocked down in the street following a too-convivial Bar dinner. The first time he roared at me, I literally jumped with fright. Fierce grey eyes glared at me from a face made more fearsome by blue overnight stubble and a black eye. 'I'm not your Daddy. Don't let me ever hear you call me that again . . . On second thoughts, address me as you please,' he said ingratiatingly. 'You're pretty enough to get away with anything.' Then he let out another roar. 'Damn and blast those women! Where have they hidden my teeth?'

Finally, his wife, the grey slim ghost of a beautiful woman, came to take him home. As they left the ward she turned back and whispered to me, 'Thank you, Nurse, you did so much for him and he is all I have.'

I still have the copy of Fitzgerald's *Omar Khayyam* she slipped into my hand. Inside the book was written the one word – 'Thanks' – and her name. Ward 15 lost one of its most colourful characters as the door closed behind him. Certainly a broken leg had not been enough to dampen his exuberant personality.

With the strings and stripes of a junior staff nurse, the housemen and students recognized me as someone they could ask to assist them; someone they could chat up if Sister was not around.

One student in particular added a pleasant flutter to the work of the ward. We had a patient with terminal cancer of the throat. Tubes had to be sterilized and changed, and he had to be fed directly into the alimentary tract. This particular student, Barry Schwartz, used to come along to do it. He was South

African, sandy haired, with cheerful blue eyes in a plain, square face. I liked to help him with his tube changing behind the red screens. And Mr Somers, the patient, welcomed the two of us with what he could muster of a smile.

'How about a ring for you, Nurse?' asked Barry. He was a dentist back home and had brought a lump of dental gold with him from Africa. He was amusing himself by making rings for his friends.

Mr Somers nodded his grey head approvingly. You could tell he was pleased to be part of this conspiracy. I really believe we two and our harmless flirtation lightened the last weeks of his life. Barry deftly replaced the tracheotomy tube.

'Now, Mr S, you watch this.' He took one of my hands and measured the circumference of the little finger with a strip of sticking plaster.

A week later, the three of us once again shut in behind the red screens, Barry slipped a signet ring on my finger. Mr Somers softly clapped his emaciated hands.

Would it have become a romance? I doubt it, except in our patient's imagination. Anyway, fate took a hand, and two days later I went sick with German measles.

21

If the question of women's suffrage left us apathetic, we four
were conscious of our new responsibility and status as staff
nurses and began to disucss the bettering of conditions for all
nurses. Symonds came out with the blunt statement, 'We're
being exploited.'

'Women doctors are fighting for recognition,' added Maxwell.
'The words "dedication" and "vocation" have kept the word
"exploitation" under wraps too long.'

We felt clear about what our demands would be – an eight-
hour day (instead of the more usual fourteen) and better pay –
but what could four insignificant juniors accomplish? We
needed a lot of support, and we could not run the risk of being
identified. Then Symonds had an idea.

'A round robin, that's the answer. Look—' She picked up a
pencil and drew a circle on the page of her note book. Then she
drew a smaller circle within, and wrote our four names, like the
spokes of a wheel radiating outwards. 'You see? Simple. This
way no-one can lay a finger on the ringleader. A coward's way
out? Perhaps, but no-one is going to throw away these years of
training. The authorities may guess who started the petition,
but a round robin tells no tales. We'll have to get every
signature possible, and that won't be easy. I think Maxwell and
I had better tackle the staff nurses,' she continued. 'We are
older than you two, and tougher. Nurses in their last year will
be afraid to tumble at the last lap.'

'The pros won't be all that happy either,' I said. 'They are
scared most of the time anyway, and this will seem like a
revolution.'

'Which it is,' was Symonds' dry retort. 'You wait and see, this
is only the beginning.' She picked up her pencil again. 'Now,'
she told us, 'we have to state our case and send it as a letter.
One copy to Matron and one to the Board of Governors.'

We wrote our letter and then set about collecting signatures.

143

The response was better than we hoped, but it was hard work arguing the shaky ones into signing. In the end, however, there were few refusals. 'Registered post,' said Symonds firmly.

So we cast our fly over the troubled waters of the nursing world. It seemed a long, long time before we got our catch, but when it came – the eight-hour day – it was our hospital which led the way, or so we liked to believe. That was a first step. And today, unbelievably, a nurse's union.

Sometimes I dream. I see a dumpy blue ghost trotting up out of the past: 'A union? Rubbish. We *are* a union – united in serving these sick and silly people. You tell me your sort of union means we can strike to better ourselves. Ourselves? Not them? Wipe that lipstick off, Nurse. And do you call that a uniform? And how do you tuck your hair under that ridiculous flyaway thing perched on top of your head? I suppose you are a nurse, and not just an ornament?'

Off trots the blue ghost who taught me how to scrub. And I wake from my dream to the security of the National Health Service, of which Sister Jane and her contemporaries were the everlasting foundation.

Hypothermia we call it today. From November to March, the new probationers fought it off with hot-water bottles, hot cocoa and hot baths. Even our young blood became chilled in the New Nurses' Home. More important, therefore, than the status of our new strings and stripes, was our removal to the Old Home in the hospital building. Here elderly radiators gurgled and rumbled, creating an atmosphere of warmth and relaxation.

When the great day of transfer arrived, I decided on a house-warming for my new quarters. As we all assembled in my room to celebrate, Symonds said, 'There's a moon tonight. I hope the sirens don't break things up.' The Zeppelin raids had been more frequent of late.

'Just in case,' said Wharton, coming in with cocoa in an enamel saucepan, her fair hair twisted up in curlers, 'let's eat and drink up. I got a pot of jam from home and made sandwiches in the ward.'

'What are we planning to do after finals?' asked Maxwell.

'That depends on the war, doesn't it?' Symonds reached for another sandwich as she spoke. And at that moment the sirens broke in with their screaming summons. We looked at one another in dismay.

'Well, that's it.' Symonds got up from her seat on the floor. 'Come on girls, down to the basement – and bring your pillows.' She hitched her woollen dressing gown around her with a determined tug and tied the cord as if she had it round the Kaiser's neck.

Annoyance, rather than fear, was the prevailing emotion in the mixed assembly in the bowels of the hospital. We talked, we yawned, we grumbled. I looked around. There was McSweeney, in a corner by herself, huddled in a worn and shabby raincoat. Symonds whispered, 'Do you know, I'm sorry for the poor devil. I worked with her for a week in Ward 5. It really impressed me to see how well she managed those sick babies.' As she spoke, she manoeuvred toward the maverick in the corner. Well, why not, I thought; the greatest of these is charity.

As Symonds' solid figure angled itself beside her, McSweeney drew back and shut her eyes. 'Come off it, McSweeney, we're all in this together.' The bright blue eyes were smiling as she nudged the shrinking figure. 'Take a chocolate.'

McSweeney opened her eyes, hesitated, and then took one. 'Thanks,' she muttered, still unsmiling and wary, but no longer with sullen rejection written on her face. Gradually Symonds drew her into conversation.

The talking and yawning and grumbling went on interminably, and then it happened. A bomb fell, and seemed to splinter all around us. No panic, but hand sought for hand. And, miraculously, University Hospital stood intact. There was a sigh of relief; quite an audible moment of thankfulness for a near miss. How near a miss would become apparent the next morning, when we saw the huge gaping hole in the road just beyond us.

Night Sister appeared. 'I want volunteers,' she said, 'to calm the patients. Come as you are. Go to your own wards – they need you.'

We all got up. Symonds held out a hand to McSweeney. 'Come, you and I are going to Ward 5.'

* * *

145

The four years of war and the three years of my training ended in November of 1918. But it was that autumn that we had another enemy on our hands – Spanish flu.

We had little with which to fight such a deadly virus: linseed poultices, cough linctuses, pneumonia jackets, and stimulants such as brandy. We were fighting with straws, not swords, and we had to stand back and watch our patients die.

I was working in one of our two military wards. We now took cot cases into the hospital and staffed the college opposite, temporarily converted into a base for convalescent soldiers. One of my patients was Private Watkins, in Bed 7. He had come home on compassionate leave, and was due to return to the front when he fell victim to Spanish flu. He was a civilian who had volunteered in the early days during the wave of patriotism that swept the country. He had come through the hell across the Channel unscathed – only to face this.

It was 11 November. I came on duty at 7 a.m., as usual, and walked straight over to his bed. I felt the already weak and erratic pulse. There were screens round his bed to shut him off from the busy life of the ward. The girl he had told me he planned to marry – 'Come the end of the war, Nurse' – sat beside his bed. She held one limp hand in hers, while silent tears ran down her cheeks. The oxygen cylinder was drawn up beside his bed. The fight was nearly over. Every breath was a painful gasp.

She got up as I wheeled the cylinder into position. 'I'll come back later, Nurse.'

The morning dragged on. And then, suddenly, it seemed as if every church bell in the great city went mad – the same bells that had been silent for four years. The Armistice had been signed. The war was over. I looked at Private Watkins. Did I imagine the flicker in his glazed eyes? I picked up his hand. There was no pulse to be found, and I went to find Sister.

I have wondered so often since then whether he heard those bells. Or perhaps he had found his own particular peace. Apart from that one still and silent figure, the whole world broke into wild jubilation. Never had such madness been known before.

The next day I received my final certificate from Matron. I was a qualified nurse – a Lady of the Lamp. Yet as I walked down the slope from Casualty, and the mingled incense of ether and carbolic floated past, I felt the sadness of a great farewell.

22

Home. Back to the 'mean little house' which I had grown to love. Yet after a few weeks with no definite objective in sight, I began to feel frustrated and decided to try private nursing.

My first moment of disillusionment came when I went to be interviewed by the matron of a nursing home in Baker Street. I was very conscious of an atmosphere of worldliness. The ideals and austerity of my training school had not prepared me for this first glimpse of a gilded cage – the soft carpets and gay chintzes for the patients of the Harley Street specialists, whose consulting rooms were only about a stone's throw away. That the matron who interviewed me wore make-up seemed the most disturbing item in the whole setup. Suddenly I became aware of a darn in the finger of one of my white cotton gloves. And yet I was also aware of a tingling of excitement. I would see another face of nursing if I was taken on. This brisk, worldly, sharp-featured woman could rub a bit of sophistication on to me.

So I accepted the terms laid down by the carefully modulated voice, and a week later I took up the new challenge.

The nursing home was two three-storeyed houses knocked into one. There were two front doors with stucco porticos; one was for doctors and patients and was gay with evergreens in tubs and baskets of flowers swinging overhead; the other, unadorned, was for use by the staff, and there was also a basement entrance marked 'Tradesmen'.

There were five resident nurses and a matron. The nurses were a mixed bunch; all were a good deal older than I, and, as I was to discover, their nursing image had become frayed at the edges by years of scyophantic nursing. The patient accommodation consisted of six luxuriously furnished rooms. Most of the patients were medical cases; hypochondria was a gold mine for our Harley Street physicians. But there was also a small, well-equipped theatre on the top floor.

My first patient was Mrs Sparrow, a cosy little woman in her early fifties. She appeared to be enjoying a prolonged convalescence after the removal of gallstones. There was very little to do for her – I could forget my nursing skills. Instead, I arranged flowers – her whole room was like a well-stocked florist's shop; I ushered in her numerous friends; and I checked her meal trays and carried them up to her, staying to chat if she was alone.

My still naïve idealism was shaken by another aspect of private nursing which I discovered from my cynical colleagues in the duty room. When patients left they were counted upon to give a present to the nurse who had looked after them. Not money – that would have been degrading, unethical – but a trinket, a bottle of exotic perfume – these things were professionally acceptable.

It was hard for me to adjust to these ideas. When Mrs Sparrow, her pretty little face looking for my pleased reaction, presented me with a gold brooch watch, I drew back, blushing and embarrassed. 'No, please, I can't.'

'But you must, Nurse, you've done so much for me – it's a sort of forever "thank you". Please.'

I took the watch, but I felt guilty. I was a traitor to all those women who had trained me to be a nurse. It was a long time before I could bring myself to wear that watch. As I took it, I dreaded the barrage of questions I would have to stand up to in the duty room.

The duty room was at the end of a long corridor. A glass case showed the numbered bells which hung on the wall to summon us at the need, or whim, of our patients. There were generally two or three of us sitting around in that small room, talking, knitting, writing letters, grumbling about life in general, or about one's individual bad luck or unfair treatment.

I was younger and less experienced in the ways of this world, so I was not, as a rule, included in these exchanges and current gossip. Also, I spent my off duty with no reference to the other nurses, which I think they took to be a kind of snobbery. I was a misfit, and I grew restless. This was certainly not what I wanted. It was 'Queenie' who forced my hand.

We nurses slept in the basement; two in one room, three in another. There was no privacy. In training school, my room was cold and austere, but my own, a place of retreat and sanctuary. I felt the instant fear and dislike stiffening my face when I found

'Queenie', who had just joined the staff, stowing away her belongings in the other set of drawers.

'Hallo, dear,' she greeted me, 'just the two of us, I see. I like that, yes, I like it very much.' Her little eyes glinted with an emotion I could not understand. It was like the face of a greedy child who has just been given a cream bun. Queenie was a lesbian, but my sheltered upbringing had left me quite ignorant of this phenomenon of nature.

The others, I feel sure, realized this from the moment Queenie entered the duty room. For them, she was an open book. I realize now that her advances to me were a source of amusement for them. The thigh-rubbing when she plumped down beside me on the shabby divan, the furtive hand feeling for contact – the picture seems so clear today, but then I could only feel an inexplicable and growing sense of fear.

The day she crawled into my bed and threw her arms around me, was the finish. I gave in my resignation, packed my case, and left that nursing home in Baker Street with no regrets. As my train pulled out of Charing Cross station, I felt as if I had climbed out of a slimy pond.

Between 1918 and 1920, as the saying goes, I rested on my oars. I let the stream of life flow by me, enjoying the security and sense of achievement that came with my status as a trained nurse. I visited here and there; I took Nanny, now crippled with arthritis, to Droitwich for the supposedly curative baths. But more importantly, I got to know my mother.

I sensed her need of me now that the mainspring of her life was broken. For the stark truth was that Richard Austin Freeman no longer needed her. Through all the years of our childhood and adolescence, she had combined her friendship with him – which created and launched his books – with our welfare and education. An education based on their own unconventional standards and planned according to the demands of his career as a writer. But now the honeymoon was over – if it ever had been that. He was famous with the launching of the Dr Thorndyke books, and fame brought him friends from all over the world and a tight circle of local admirers.

My mother and I never discussed the relationship, which was so important to her, but one day, I realized with horror the role

I was taking on. I was rapidly becoming the indispensable 'dutiful daughter'.

That day I bought a copy of a nursing paper and scanned its back pages for a suitable position. Perhaps a job in Florence, or the French Riviera? At all costs, I must get away – splash my life with colour – find romance.

Part Four
Cairo

23

A letter from Cuthbert proved to be the springboard to my future. He wrote from Cairo:

> *The matron of the Anglo-American Hospital here is a friend of mine. If you like, she will be happy to take you on her staff. But she says you'll have to pass your midwifery exam first. I have been seconded from my regiment to learn Arabic, and I'm toying with the idea of applying for an administrative job in the Soudan. Hurry up. Come out while I'm still here.*

This was it. My chance. And I took it. With a certificate of training from a London teaching hospital, one could become a certified midwife in three months. I lost no time. I signed forms, went for interviews, and started my training in the old Queen Mary's Maternity Home on Hampstead Heath.

The building had once been the home of Lord Leverhulme, the soap king, and was not well adapted for a hospital. But we got by. We were a small, cheerful community. Most of us had recently escaped from the rigid etiquette of training schools and were enjoying the freedom and camaraderie of our new status. There was a light-hearted, schoolgirl element to our daily routine, so that a daily chore, like bathing babies, became a competition for speed. The slippery little bodies were washed and dressed before their mothers had even missed them.

My first experience of the Labour Ward came after two weeks. 'There is always a first time,' said the Sister, with more kindness than originality, as we got into our overalls and scrubbed up. My nervousness must have been obvious to her observant eyes. I had had little contact with the 'birds and bees' aspect of life, and birth came as a very stark truth.

The babies delivered in textbooks and fairy tales had lacked that fourth dimension of unlovely reality. But as I manipulated my first infant out of its mother's womb, I sensed that reality, in this case, was more exciting and wonderful than any fairy tale. Out of all the pain and blood and mess, I felt the thrill and glory of creation as I cut the umbilical cord.

'Don't stand gaping,' snapped Sister, and there was a subdued giggle from fellow students who had come for the demonstration. She took the baby from me and gave it to one of the group: 'You can bathe him, Nurse Jones, and don't forget the eyes.' Then she turned to me. 'You and I will clean up here,' she said, 'and by the time we're through you can deal with the afterbirth.' It was back to earth with a jolt, but it was a first time to remember. And first times are what we always do remember; they stand out as sharp as noonday shadows.

Each of us had to deliver twenty babies before we could sit the exam. We were also supposed to spend two weeks working in the slums of the East End. This switch to 'the district' was the real test of our skills and resources. Armed with our official black bags, we would face a challenge greater than that faced by St George when we battled with dirt, infection and ignorance. However, it was difficult to fit us all into the schedule, and another girl and I found ourselves delivering our twentieth atom of humanity without undergoing this trial.

The Nemesis descended. We had an official visit from the great Dr Fairbanks, whose book on midwifery had been our bible. 'He's here,' the whisper went round. 'He's going to do a round.' We students had to trail around the wards after the great man, while Matron trotted beside him. At the end of his inspection and questioning, he rounded on the poor woman, a rosy-faced Scottish woman, whose cheeks were paler than usual during this ordeal.

'Do I understand,' he said, in deliberate, icy tones, 'that there are two students here who are leaving shortly and will sit for the Central Midwives Board Examination *without* going on the district?'

'Yes, Sir,' mumbled Matron, and her face flushed with embarrassment.

'And what do they really know? Of what use would they be if faced with the problems of a slum area?' The unfortunate woman could only stammer out excuses.

However, I had successfully answered his textbook questions with textbook answers, and a few weeks later I sat the exam and passed. I had the certificate I wanted, and by the quickest and easiest means. I had no desire to practice as a midwife, and I was thankful to have escaped the two weeks on the district. The policeman on his beat may have known more about emergency deliveries than I, but I could write CMB after my name, and that was all I needed – my passport to the Golden East.

There was no flying in those days. Instead the ships of the P&O line ploughed their stately way through enchanted waters – east and west. I walked up the gangway of the great ship feeling as though I had my feet on Jacob's ladder. There was little money in my purse and few dresses in my pressed-cane trunk, but I was happy. My whole life was now in focus; I had only to press the bulb to make the perfect picture.

What a fantastic translation! From the 'mean little house' in Clarence Place to this floating centre of amusement and, it seemed to me, luxury. I thought it had come cheap at the price of those three gruelling years of training. Nothing could spoil my enjoyment of every moment. Even a few days of bad weather which emptied the dining saloon did not affect me.

I shared a cabin with a girl who was going on to India to be married. Love and romance were rammed down my throat every night and every morning, and I began to wonder whether I myself was ever going to be caught up in this obsession again. I had been under the spell for a while, with Desmond Nolan, but much of that had just been a youthful falling in love with love.

'Come on, let's go to the bar for a drink.' My roommate took hold of my arm. 'You're a bit of a dreamer, aren't you? Well, on this ship we have to be doing things all the time.'

She was right, I thought, as the randy old colonel with the bristling white moustache bought me a second pink gin. I had walked up that gangway into a social whirlpool. I remembered Lily Mason's directive: 'You cannot sit at my luncheon table and say nothing; you must learn to talk, to listen, to sparkle.' I had had my first lessons in her villa in Fiesole, and I was adapting well to this heady atmosphere of fun and frivolity.

All too soon (or was I becoming a little bit bored with all of this?) there was the last dance, the scribbling down of names and addresses, and then we were docking alongside the old pontoon bridge at Port Said. We crowded to the rails, looking for friends and relatives amongst the swarm of small boats bobbing about on the blue water below. Suddenly, an invading army of skinny brown forms in garish cotton robes scrambled up the rope ladders, leather goods, brasses, rugs and silks on their backs. I was caught up in the middle of a frenzy of sales talk and was beginning to feel a wave of homesickness, when I caught sight of Cuthbert's assured, stocky form coming toward me. My relief and pleasure were spontaneous.

Together, we crossed the desert to Cairo by train, and then drove over the great Kasr el Nil Bridge to the island of Gezira.

24

As we got out of the rickety carriage that had brought us to our journey's end, I stood still for a few minutes, taking in the scene before me. We had come down a road bordered by tall jacaranda trees, their pale blue blossoms lighting up the deep green foliage. The hospital itself was set back from the road, a low white building decorated by trailing branches of purple bougainvillea.

Cuthbert, having directed the driver to wait, turned to me. 'Like it?' he asked. He pointed to a green stretch of grass across the road. 'The Sporting Club,' he told me. 'You nurses are honorary members.'

The matron, a gently fluttering dove dressed in grey, welcomed us into her pleasant sitting room, where the decor was English, except for the highly polished brass table set before the chintz-covered divan. 'I hope you'll be happy here with us, Miss Bishop,' she said in a soft, kindly voice. 'We are a small community, so we have to fit in well together.' Before she finished speaking, she added, 'Sit here beside me, and Captain Bishop can sit in that rocking chair opposite. I happen to know he likes that chair.'

She rang a small brass bell that was on the table in front of her. A native servant appeared, red tarbush on his head, scarlet sandals showing beneath his long white robe, and she gave him orders in fluent Arabic.

'Few of my nurses trouble to learn the language,' she said. 'The servants in this hospital get by with a good understanding of the orders we give them.'

This will be a very different aspect of private nursing, I thought, recalling the Home in Baker Street; I think I'm going to enjoy it.

Then the servant reappeared with tea, just as we served it at home – silver teapot and delicate white china. After the oppressive heat of the sunbaked world outside, it felt cool in this quiet room where the air was stirred by a fan set high up in the ceiling.

The Matron questioned me about my nursing experiences, and she and Cuthbert gave me a picture of life as it was lived in the Anglo-American colony of which I was now a part. Then Cuthbert looked at his watch. 'I must go,' he said. 'I have a session with my sheikh at six o'clock.'

'I will show your sister around her new home,' said Matron as we all walked toward the door.

And so began my life in the Anglo-American Hospital on the island of Gezira, that seeming paradise of greenery splashed with the brilliant orange of the hellfire creeper, the purple of the irrepressible bougainvillea, and the beautiful blue blossoms of the jacaranda. But the houseboats moored all round the island were infested by rats, and the menace of dysentery and typhoid lurked even in the leaves of a freshly washed lettuce.

We were really more of a nursing home than a hospital, a small community of a dozen or so nursing sisters with a few native orderlies to help with our male patients. Each of us was responsible to a doctor for the treatment of his patient. We dressed in white floating army veils giving us an almost nun-like appearance. But with the Sporting Club across the road and the racecourse just beyond we were not tempted to lead a cloistered life. We emerged from the chrysalis of our uniform to hover like butterflies on the outskirts of Cairo society.

I felt at home from my very first day. Partly, I think, because I knew that Cuthbert was at the other end of a telephone. And also because, at the beginning of my new life, I found a friend.

One evening, shortly after I arrived, I wandered out into the grounds of the hospital and was debating whether I could summon the nerve to cross the road to the Sporting Club and explore its possibilities, when there was a light touch on my arm. I turned and saw the smiling face of Gladys Thackray. She had sat beside me at lunch and had managed to make me feel at ease then, helping me, with her unobtrusive prompting, to join in the talk. She had a square-built figure and was plain, almost to ugliness. But when she spoke to you, you were aware only of the warm beauty of her smile.

'I know what you're thinking,' she said. 'I felt the same myself, my first week here. Why don't we go over to the Club together. We can look around, and I'll introduce you to some of the members. Do you play bridge?'

I shook my head. 'I'm afraid not.'

'Pity, but there are other things you can join in. Come on, let's not waste any more time.'

And that was the beginning of a friendship that eased me into my new life before I had time to feel homesick. I began, again, to feel like a cork bobbing on the sunlit water of a quiet harbour.

I spent a great deal of my off-duty time with Cuthbert. He had not much use for the insular outlook and the amusements that occupied the leisure hours of the government officials, the army contingent from the Citadel, and the Residency staff and their wives. Instead, he would hire a ramshackle car, and we would make expeditions beyond the closed circle of the Anglo-American community.

He took me to the Mousky, the native bazaar, where we drank little cups of black coffee with a bearded Egyptian, whose bald head was protected from the hot rays of the sun by a turban. The Egyptian sat cross-legged on the mud floor while we sat on wooden stools and he displayed the brass goods that shone like gold in the dark interior of his crowded booth. The fortune-teller's scratching in the sand, the 'gulla gulla' man with his chickens, the braying of the donkeys laden with baskets of watermelon – the variety of sights, sounds, and smells was bewildering and exciting.

Cuthbert flicked an inquisitive goat out of our way with a fly switch which most people carried in Egypt, for flies were more than just a nuisance here, they were a menace. I shuddered when I saw them black on the faces of the native children.

'I think I'll try out my Arabic on that letter-writer,' he said. 'He's the genuine article, not bait for the tourists like the others.' He indicated a white robed scribe bending over a rickety desk and taking dictation from an old woman wearing a yashmak.

Indeed, I believe what Cuthbert enjoyed most when we went to the Mousky were his short dialogues with the people. 'A lot of it is bogus,' he told me, 'put on for the tourist, but here and there you find the real Egypt. You see that fellow over there with the handful of postcards?'

'Yes,' I said. 'He would give a crocodile indigestion.'

159

'Well, you go on ahead and show interest in that fruit stall – haggle over a watermelon. While your back is turned, he'll slide up to me and try to sell me his dirty postcards. And I'm going to give him a broadside in his native tongue.'

Another day we rattled along the road to the Pyramids and the Sphinx. But we did not lunch at the Mena House Hotel; we ate sandwiches and drank beer in the sunken garden of the Greek restaurant opposite it. And we looked up at the Sphinx and the Great Pyramid and remembered the days when Richard Austin Freeman held forth on the greatness that was the Egypt of the pharaohs.

Yet, for me, something was missing. The romance that is the spice of life when one is young. 'You should marry,' said Cuthbert, in his forthright way, as he set his tankard down on the wooden table. He looked at me thoughtfully. 'You're a good-looker, but somehow I think you are missing out on something. Perhaps the window-dressing isn't quite right.'

Deep down I knew that he was right. I remembered the romantic poems hidden away in a box at home. I thought of my brief encounter with Desmond Nolan, the dour Irishman who walked into my life and out again. 'If I had married,' I told Cuthbert, 'I would have missed all this. And come to think of it – why haven't you married?'

'Ask the Sphinx,' he retorted, and we both laughed.

Another day we climbed the Great Pyramid and rode camels with the tourists, who insisted that a camel ride was a must. Cuthbert mounted his kneeling camel with tolerant amusement. 'Reminds me of those donkey rides on Margate sands.'

'Even to the boy with the stick,' I said, settling myself on the mountain of flesh.

But all too soon, Cuthbert was recalled. I wept as his train pulled out of the station. He leaned out of the open window. 'Get a replacement – for keeps,' he said.

Easier said than done, I thought sadly, as I turned away.

With Cuthbert gone, I realized how little contact I would have with this country in which I was living and working. The superimposed culture of the West would once more absorb me; Egypt, with its unique past and its mixed-up present, was out of the reach of a British nurse marooned on an island dominated by imperial colonialism.

In the hospital, the servants – the domestic staff, the orderlies who looked after our male patients – were Egyptian. Taha, the head orderly, ruled his little kingdom, submitting to the orders of the English sisters, who for the most part gave the orders in their own tongue. But across the road was our home from home, the Sporting Club, with its racecourse, polo ground, golf course and tennis courts – all strictly for Anglo-American enjoyment. The rulers of the Protectorate needed these compensations for exile.

One day I voiced my feelings to Gladys Thackray. 'It's all wrong,' I said as we sat on the flat roof looking across at the spread of greenery that was the Club. 'I might have been brought up on Kipling, but surely by now things should have changed.'

Gladys picked up the golf bag propped beside her and her slow, warm smile preceded her reply. 'It's not going to last,' she said. 'The cracks are beginning to show. Enjoy it while you can. The gulla gulla man with his chickens will be the only one to miss us when we go. See you later, and don't forget we have an Egyptian patient coming in this evening, and this one will be a shock to our insularity.'

I nodded as I walked back to the duty room. 'East is East and West is West,' I told myself, and the cliché seemed to fit, for our Egyptian patient was a young girl from a rich family who was to be operated on by our Dr Dobbin, who had a worldwide reputation as a gynaecologist.

I thought of the young girl who would be occupying the flower-filled room at the end of the corridor. A virgin by compulsion; Islamic Egypt taking no chances. I had come a long way from the days of my training when Symonds told me 'You still have a lot of eggshell sticking to you,' but this crude enforcement of virginity was a revelation that revolted me. The idea of the stitched vaginal labia which had to be opened up by a surgeon's knife before a marriage could be consummated shook my ideals and made me question the relationship between lust and romance.

Restless and unhappy, I walked out on to the roof again. My convalescent patient was with friends and I was to help Matron out with the state visit of the Matron and senior Sisters from the native Hospital, Kasr el Aini, for we even ran their hospital for them.

161

When they arrived, I looked down on the quartet of army caps fluttering below in the light breeze as they alighted from their carriage drawn up to our front door. Protocol brought back to mind, I tweaked my own cap into decorous folds and hurried downstairs.

25

It was Gladys Thackray's patient who was the mother of the Bader twins; their father was the American consul in Cairo at that time. When he first saw the twins, each like a little mummy in a blue bedsock, he ejaculated one word: 'Gosh!' Poor fellow, the twins were his to be cherished, but his young wife was slipping away on a wave of pain and suffering. She lay dying in a room upstairs, a grey shadow of the girl he had married and brought out to Egypt a short while ago. Tuberculosis, in its most virulent form (popularly known as 'galloping consumption'), was going to rob him of a wife, and the twins of a mother.

We all felt involved in this tragedy. It hung like a cloud of sadness over our full and busy lives. Matron did not encourage 'shop talk', but even her restraining presence at meals could not keep us silent on the subject of the Bader family.

Two weeks after the birth of the twins, Matron sent for me. She was seated behind her desk, a nun-like figure with grey hair parted in the middle, her face framed like that of a madonna by the grey silk folds of her cap. A plain gold cross hung on a thin gold chain, rising and falling with her quiet breathing. What could she have known of love and passion, of destructive grief or jealousy or fear? And yet, I felt convinced, she knew it all. She laid aside her pen.

'As you know,' she said, 'Miss Thackray has been Mrs Bader's special nurse on night duty. But now Miss Thackray has gone sick. She asked me, this morning, to let you go in her place. There is nothing we can do to save Mrs Bader's life, but if we can help her through the last hours of suffering, it will be something deeply worthwhile. Are you willing to do it?'

'Yes, Matron,' I said.

'Then you will go on special duty tonight. I believe it is only a matter of hours before the end, so be prepared.'

I turned my head to look out of the window at the green grass of the Sporting Club and the racecourse beyond, the focal points of the social circle to which the dying girl had belonged. She had been one of the gay young-marrieds, enjoying this faraway fragment of the life she had felt behind.

'I will do my best, Matron,' I assured her stiffly, afraid I might betray the involvement I was feeling.

She smiled one of her rare smiles. 'I know you will.'

As I left the office, the dying girl's husband rushed by me in the corridor, a pale-faced young man whose horn-rimmed glasses somehow emphasized the look of tension and distress that were obvious, even to a casual passer-by. I don't believe he noticed I was there.

After lunch I went to my room. I bathed, pulled the curtains to darken the room to an illusion of evening, got under the mosquito net, and laid my head on the pillow. But the routine non-involvement advice of my training days had never worked for me. I dreaded the coming night's vigil. Thackray must have felt much the same, for when I roused from my uneasy dozing I found a note slipped under my door, which read: *She needs prayer as much as nursing; even more than nursing*.

At 8 o'clock we assembled in the duty room, as usual. Matron was there, seated at a table to outline the night's work for us. The report book was open in front of her. It was all friendly and informal.

She left my assignment to the last, till we were alone. We looked at each other for a couple of minutes without speaking. Then she said, 'As I told you this morning, Sister, I doubt if Mrs Bader will last the night out.' She turned to the dressing trolley beside her and handed me a metal dish, which held a hypodermic syringe and two small bottles. I had no need to read the labels; one was morphia, the other a heart stimulant.

When I entered the sickroom I found my patient sleeping. The youthful face was grey and ravaged beneath the crimson patch that highlighted each cheekbone. The disease had swept through her as swiftly as a fire sweeps through a forest. The nine months of pregnancy had masked the earlier symptoms. The twins, snug and warm in their mother's womb, had been blamed when things did not seem to be normal in her pregnancy. No-one had suspected the truth until it was too late.

I pulled the mosquito net aside. Softly, I drew the sweat-stained hair away from her face. I soaked a tissue in some cologne water that stood on the bedside table and laid it on the burning skin. When she woke, it would be to pain and agony.

Should I give her the stimulant that would prolong that useless suffering? Who was I to be the assessor – to weigh the scales now balanced precariously between life and death? I pulled a curtain aside and stared out on a starlit sky. It only stared back at me – no help, no inspiration there. And yet, beyond the stars, I must believe there was God in His Heaven.

I let the curtain fall and turned back to the room. I checked the wildly erratic ups and down of her chart. Pulse and temperature records, what did they matter now? I would have to come to a decision soon. Standing beside her bed, watching her troubled sleep, I asked myself if I was going to usurp the power of God.

A sigh escaped from the pale lips. 'Dear Lord,' I prayed, 'let the decision be yours.'

She was awake now, her eyes wide but unseeing. I looked again at the syringe, the two bottles. Was I a coward? Was I failing a human being in distress? Her pain was returning. I noted the creased brow, the twisted, froth-rimmed lips, and picked up the morphia. 'Merciful God, take over.'

She tried to raise herself. Weak and exhausted, she cried out, 'No, no, let me die.' I opened the bottle and filled the syringe. I felt calm, the calmness of despair. There would be no help from heaven; the decision must be mine.

But even as I bent to give the injection, she fell back with a cough that sent spatters of blood on to her pillow. Our prayers had been answered.

26

September, with its humid heat, had left us all feeling drained of energy. But the Sporting Club provided relaxation and amusement: croquet, golf, tennis, and long cool drinks at sundown.

There was a lighter side to life in the Anglo-American Hospital, and to that side belonged Cousin William. Several of us were chatting in the duty room one afternoon, when someone asked, 'Didn't you say your mother's name was Maule?' I nodded assent, looking up from a letter I was writing home. 'Well, there's a new patient along the corridor says he must be a cousin of yours, a William Maule. The real sugar daddy type – look out.' There was a general laugh.

Self-styled Cousin William turned out to be paunchy, red-faced, and in his late fifties. He had a roving eye, but he also had a sharp-tongued American wife called Caroline who fought a losing battle against this tendency of his to philander. There was no real harm in him; he was just a nuisance to the younger members of the nursing staff.

One day Caroline persuaded me to take her up on to the flat roof, where two or three deck chairs were set out for the use of our convalescents. I had shown immunity to Cousin William's charm, and so his wife felt she could unload her grievances on me.

'That Sporting Club is just too handy for his little games,' she complained. 'All those hedges! And girls like that no-good Phyllis Butt, lying in wait for soppy fools like him.' She sighed, and opening her large crocodile handbag, she took out a cigarette case that could only have been bought in the Mousky. 'What has that girl got that I haven't got?' she continued. 'And a bit over.' She patted her ample bosom, hung with strings of beads. 'Platonic,' she snorted, tossing her hennaed head till her pendant earrings danced. 'It starts that way, but that platonic business doesn't throw any dust in my eyes. An affair is an affair, and it always ends below the waist!'

166

But Cousin William was not all lecherous in his attitude to women. I went on night duty a few days before he left, and during my round of settling the patients he was always ready for a chat. One night I complained to him about my trouble getting to sleep. A couple of days later he sent me a case of beer, accompanied by a card that read: *Take one at bedtime; better than any of the stuff they dish out in the hospital.*

The noise that came from the servants' quarters at all hours was something neither beer nor pills could help. I plugged my ears, I drank my beer, all to no avail. Finally, I took a stiff dose of veronal. Too stiff. I slept and slept, frightening Thackray when she could get no response from the lump under the mosquito net that was me. She went for help. By the time they finally managed to rouse me, dawn was coming up and someone else had to go on duty in my place.

One day Gladys came to me with an open letter in her hand. 'You do a lot of scribbling,' she said. 'Words seem to trickle out of your pen. Would you ever write a letter for me?'

'You make me feel like one of those scribes in the Mousky,' I smiled. 'Of course I will.'

She sat down on my bed. 'This friend of mine had a son who was killed out here in the war. He is buried in the cemetery here and she wants a description of the scene.'

'There's an Armistice Day coming up,' I said thoughtfully. 'Let's wait a few days and give her that picture.'

'That's a good idea,' she agreed, 'and I'll bring my Brownie camera.'

On that day those of us who could be spared went off with Matron to join the rest of the Anglo-American colony for the service to be held in the burial ground outside the city. The flags of the wartime Allies flapped gently against their poles, hardly stirred by the faint gusty breeze. The tall eucalyptus trees, warmed by the sun, filled the air with their astringent scent – reminders of the lurking fevers they were supposed, by the monks who planted them, to guard against. Their leaves rustled ceaselessly, a dry whispering, as twig rubbed against twig, and leaf against leaf. The sky overhead was a wash of deep blue, unbroken by clouds.

As I stood amongst this little group of exiles, I recalled the first Armistice Day – my last day in the wards at University

College Hospital. I thought of Private Watkins. Had he heard the shattering clamour of those church bells? Or, remembering the old nursery rhyme,

> *Four corners to my bed.*
> *Four angels at my head.*
> *One to watch, and one to pray,*
> *and two to bear my soul away*

I wondered whether they already borne his soul away to a peace that would last for ever.

The three minutes of silence were over. I opened my eyes. Thackray was looking at me. 'What were you whispering?' she asked.

'An old rhyme,' I told her, 'or perhaps a prayer. Or the answer to a question.' In those three minutes of silence I had relived the end of a world war, the end of my apprenticeship, and the end of a life.

'They shall not grow old, as we, who are left, grow old.' The voice of the Army chaplain rang clearly in the still air. All round us was another congregation, the silent dead we had come out to honour. Their graves were marked, each one, by a simple white cross. Each of these crosses pinpointed a loss, but also a hope: 'I am the Resurrection and the Life.'

The Last Post. Reveille.

I was close to tears now. The marching feet of the men returning to the Citadel were syncopated by the solemn sadness of the dead march, and I caught hold of Gladys' hand as we all turned away and prepared to take up the business of living once more.

'I'll write that letter tonight,' I promised.

27

Now, though unaware of it, I was heading for the rocks, the shoals, and the breakers of matrimony.

Fate is a very strange arranger of lives. Why did I have to come out to Egypt to meet my future husband, when for months he had been lying wounded in one London hospital, while I was training in another only a few miles away? But if we had met then, would the attraction have been the same? Is there perhaps not only a right person, but also a right moment?

Oliver Moriarty was not my patient, but when his nurse went off duty, I was usually the one who took over. He was a surgical case on four-hourly dressings. 'He's not a run-of-the-mill, government official type,' I was told. 'When he feels like it, he's a talker. Well, he would be – that's his trade,' his nurse added, picking up her knitting from the table in the duty room. 'He's a barrister in the Supreme Court. Nothing for you to do for him really. I'll be back for his next dressing. He very often has visitors. Look in on him now and then – he gets bored.'

That first afternoon there were no visitors, so after an hour or so I looked in on my temporary charge as directed. He was sitting up in bed with cards laid out on a tray in front of him. As I opened the door, he looked up. 'Hallo, Sister,' he greeted me. 'Do you play patience?'

I smiled. 'Double Demon and Miss Milligan.'

'Good for you,' he grinned. 'Tell me, what's your name? You've been told mine, and a lot more besides, I'll bet.'

His speaking voice had warm overtones and a trace of an Irish accent that was delightful and individual. Was this to be another Irish interlude? What nonsense! I told myself as I picked up the half-empty water carafe beside his bed. 'I'll fill this up; we've just had a delivery of ice.'

'Thanks!' As an afterthought, he added, 'And Sister, while you're about it, will you find me something to read?'

'Certainly,' I told him, 'but there's not much choice in our so-called library. I'll see what I can find.'

'Thanks, again.' And he turned back to his card game.

As I laid my hand on the handle of the door, I had a strange premonition that the choosing of that book was something special.

There was, indeed, little choice in the library. Many of the books were ephemeral romances left behind by patients because they were not worth a place on anybody's bookshelf. Others were cheap editions of the more dreary classics. Mental stimulation was what a mind like Oliver's needed, and where could I find it in this uninspiring collection?

Then, scanning the shelves, my eyes lit on the solution: Alex Munthe's *Story of San Michele*, a book I myself had read and enjoyed to the last full stop. Somehow I knew that finding this gem amongst all the rubbish was going to be important to me. I walked back to the white-walled room, its sterile atmosphere relieved only by a vase of purple bougainvillea.

As Oliver turned to take the book, our eyes met. 'I felt I could trust you,' he said, smiling. 'This is obviously not Ethel M. Dell tripe, which is all the others ever brought me.' I blushed, not from embarrassment, but because something was passing between us, a strangely significant appraisal.

Oliver was with us for quite a few weeks. Since there were no antibiotics in those days, sepsis cases such as his took time and patience to clear up. I began to look forward to the occasions when I took over for his nurse. There seemed to be so much to talk about once the barriers had been broken down by the *Story of San Michele*.

Oliver was a Kerryman, he told me, with his roots in Killarney. His father had been Clerk of the Crown Peace in the County of Kerry, a title that was washed away in the stormy waters of the troubles. Though he followed his father into the legal profession, Oliver had chosen to be a barrister rather than a solicitor.

As the patient got better, I would summon Taha, the senior orderly, to wheel him on to the flat roof of the hospital in the cool of the evening. The stories of our lives unfolded there as we talked. My insular ignorance both amazed and annoyed him.

Then one day two friends visited him, good-looking young fellows from the garrison up at the Citadel. When they left his room and I returned on a pulse- and temperature-taking mission, he announced, 'They want me for a court martial defence. Exciting! The charge is murder. Do you think old Brown will let me take it on?' The 'old Brown' referred to was his doctor.

'I don't see why not,' I replied, shaking the thermometer. 'You went to the races last week.'

There was silence as his lips clamped down on the thermometer. I took his hand. When my fingers found his pulse, an electric current seemed to pass between us. Whose heartbeat was I recording? I asked myself, as I picked up his chart and took out my pen.

The day he went off to the court martial I was again doing substitute duty. 'Wish me luck,' he said. And then he added, dropping his voice to a whisper as the two friends walked on ahead, 'Stay with me in the courtroom.'

My eyes met his. 'Do you have to ask?' For by this time I knew that I had arrived at journey's end.

It was late afternoon before the three returned. One look at Oliver's face and I knew that he had won his case. 'He's about played out,' said the elder of the two friends, 'but you should have heard him!'

'You all need a drink,' I said. 'You'll find everything on the bedside table. I'll go and get some ice.' I returned to find they had put him to bed. 'Not too long,' I warned, as I put the bowl of ice beside the glasses.

'Ten minutes, and he's all yours, Sister.'

When I came back again I found him lying, drained and exhausted. I silently put away his clothes. I held out the tussore silk suit. 'I'll have this pressed for you,' I said.

'Thanks.' He sat up in bed, and abruptly, out of the blue, he said, 'Have you ever been in love? But of course you have. Damn him! What happened! Do you still care? Come over here, please. Don't stand there like an ice maiden. Answer me – do you still care?'

Like a mechanical figure I walked towards him. 'No,' I told him. 'Not now, not for a long time.'

'Why are you not married? Why am I not married? Well, she died, that's why. Typhoid. I came home on leave for her funeral. Come nearer – give me your hand. It is you who matter now. Do you think we could make a go of life together?'

171

I felt mesmerized by the urgency in his voice and words. I held out both my hands. He pulled me towards him, but just as our lips met there was a shattering knock at the door – Matron, come to assess the damage done by the outing.

I left them together and went to supervise the setting of his supper tray. I wouldn't go back. Taha, the orderly, could do all that was needed. I needed time – to adjust, to consult with Thackray. Where was she?

'Thack,' I said, when I found her in her room, 'I think I'm about to become engaged.'

She laughed. 'You goose, you must know.' She kissed me, her warm brown eyes shining with excitement. 'Come tell me about it. Oliver Moriarty, isn't it? I've seen it coming, so you needn't be cagey with me. I'm glad it's not the young man from Irrigation who calls you Sunshine.'

I told my story.

'Of course you're engaged! This calls for celebration.' She pulled open the door of her wardrobe and produced a bottle of sherry. 'And you're right. Don't go back tonight. The calm, cold light of day is needed to finalize this. I tell you what, trust me. I'll lure Eager [Oliver's nurse] away after she has fixed him up for the day, then you go in, and good luck to you both.' She filled our glasses.

That night I went to sleep wrapped in clouds of fantasy. But morning, which brought the merciless routine of a nurse's life, gave the happenings of the night before a sense of unreality. Were we really engaged? Had I really promised to live with a man of whom I knew so little? I knew something about his childhood, about his life in Killarney with his parents and his sister. But what did I know of the Oliver of today?

I knew that he had been wounded in the war. That he had a disability pension because of a jaw held together by a silver plate – and where would a barrister be if he could not use his jaw? But what else did I know?

Absent-mindedly I spooned salt into my coffee. We were at breakfast, with Matron presiding. I got up from the table and poured myself a fresh cup. Coffee and scrambled egg seemed a prosaic beginning to the most wonderful day of my life. 'Around eleven,' whispered Thackray as we got up from the table.

Finally, the moment I both dreaded and welcomed arrived. I stood outside Oliver's door with my hand on the knob. And then – but how did it come about – I was standing beside his bed, seemingly cool and assured, and he was holding both my hands. 'You do realize that we are engaged?' he was saying.

I heard myself answer, 'Yes, I know.' The white walls of the hospital room seemed to close in round us. Life would never be the same again.

That night I wrote my letter home. They must share in my happiness. Suddenly, I felt that my mother had become the most important person in my past. I saw her there, as if she were actually present. She was sitting in her own special armchair in a corner of the room. The shaded light from an oil lamp lit up her clear-cut, classical features. 'Mother, you could be a Roman emperor,' Cuthbert once told her during a craze he had for modelling in clay. Her slender white hands were fitting an Egyptian cigarette into her long ivory holder, and then she looked across at me.

'I didn't know how to bring it about. You thought I didn't care, but I did. And now I'm so happy for you.'

It was fantastic; the illusion was so real that I found myself speaking aloud: 'Mother, stay there. Stay with me. I'm happy, but I've never felt so homesick before.' Then her image was wiped away by a burst of tears.

It was not long before Oliver was pronounced convalescent and able to return to his apartment in the city. Now our meetings were spaced out as time and circumstances permitted – between the demands of his practice and my off-duty hours. We would often meet in the Sporting Club, where the hedges Cousin Caroline had complained about gave us some measure of privacy. We dined at Shepheards; we met friends for drinks at Groppi's Garden. This was the normal social pattern of Anglo-American residents. But Oliver's perspective was wider than that of the usual government official. His clients were multi-racial, and he was comfortable everywhere.

Courtship in those days had four stages: walking; talking; engaged; married. We were entering stage three, the seal of which was set by the giving of a ring. At home, there would have been a party.

'I have something to give you,' said Oliver, as I got into the car beside him (if I was his first love, that car was his second). There was no need to tell me what he meant. We drove in

173

silence over the Kasr el Nil bridge in a restful silence of understanding and sharing.

'I sent Ali, my servant, away,' he told me, as he turned the key in the door of his apartment. 'This is our moment, and either you trust me or you don't.' He held out his hand, and as his fingers closed round mine, I knew that whatever he wanted I would surrender. And I was afraid. If I was weak enough to throw away all the ideals I have lived with, just for a few moments of bliss, what would be left? How could I be happy, living with my tarnished image?

I followed Oliver into his bedroom. He pulled the curtains across the window to subdue the glare of the afternoon sun, switched on the electric fan, and tossed his jacket on a chair. 'Don't be afraid,' he told me. 'I just want to hold you in my arms.' And so we lay there on the wide divan bed, with the noise of the city reminding us that life had to be lived, and this moment was not for ever.

Sundown! The muezzin sounding from the city's mosques. Oliver jumped up and pulled me to my feet. 'We'll drink to this moment of certainty,' he said. For that's what it was.

Back in the small clustered sitting room he mixed drinks, getting ice from an icebox in the corner of the room. Out of a timeless vacuum, we had returned to where seconds became minutes and minutes became the hours that ruled our lives. We touched glasses and drank. Then, taking my hand, he said, in his blunt, disconcerting way, 'Could I have raped you, darling?'

I nodded, a hot flush of shame dyeing my cheeks crimson.

'But I didn't. Not a bad foundation for trust, wouldn't you say? Do you know, my bit of Victoriana, you look even lovelier when you blush.' His voice changed. 'But men have made love to you before. How far did you let them go?' A sharp note of jealousy edged his words. 'Not fair – we'll bury our lurid pasts, yours as well as mine. Drink up, darling; I'll show you that something special I have for you.'

He picked up a small leather case from the table and put it into my hands. With trembling fingers I pressed the catch and lifted the lid. There, on a bed of white velvet, lay my engagement ring. Sapphires and diamonds. He lifted it out and slipped it on to my finger. 'Betrothed!' he said with a smile. 'You like it?'

'It's beautiful,' and I turned my hand to admire the sparkle of the stones.

'You seem to approve,' he teased. 'Well, from now on it tells the world you're my woman.'

Back in my room that evening, I remembered that a nurse could not wear a ring on duty. I rummaged in my small jewellery box till I found a discarded silver chain. I would wear my ring, but as a glittering secret.

As it turned out, I was more conscious of it lying between my breasts than when it was on my finger. And even a closely guarded secret can be discovered by someone interested in the holder of that secret.

The morning after the ring was put on my finger, and the song in my heart, the young man from Irrigation looked at me with quizzical appraisal. 'What's up, Sunshine?' he asked. 'A sleepless night – or a giddy one?' I shook up the thermometer and held it out to him.

He was fair-haired, pink-cheeked and blue-eyed, a typical mother's darling. But a small moustache gave a touch of masculinity to his otherwise baby face. In the duty room we had decided that he was looking for a wife in a desultory way, sifting the chaff from the wheat, as it were. There was not a great deal of choice in the small community that shared his social outlook. Most of the young women were newly-marrieds.

'Neither,' I answered coldly. 'Keep your lips closed, or that thermometer won't register. And—' I picked up his hand to take his pulse '—if Matron was to hear you call me Sunshine, there wouldn't be any for me.'

'Sorry,' he mumbled, 'but you are, you know.' As I removed the thermometer from his mouth, he caught sight of the silver chain. 'Come clean, what's on the end of that chain?' he challenged.

Why did I always have to give myself away by blushing? I pulled the ring from its hiding place, and its glitter seemed to mock him as it swung before his eyes.

'Another hope gone down the drain,' he said quietly. 'Lucky man.'

175

28

Wedding plans – what fun if I had been at home. There were letters, of course, and a cable and cheques. But the thrill of the wrapped parcel shared with my mother and Nanny; the friends like Babs Standfield and Daisy Burridge, to giggle and exclaim – these I missed.

We planned a wedding in two parts: a civil ceremony at the British Consulate and a short service in the Catholic cathedral. For this last, the clergy were demanding our baptismal certificates. Mine was easy to produce, but there appeared to be no hope of one for Oliver, the troubles in Ireland meant that many such records had been destroyed. But without this bit of paper, the hierarchy refused to marry us.

'Will you not accept an affidavit?' suggested Oliver, the lawyer.

The pompous little priest shook his head. 'It would not be permitted,' he said, in careful English. Then I had one of my bright ideas.

'Right, Father,' said I, making for the door. 'We will consider ourselves married when we leave the British Consul's office, and we shall live in sin.' Before his consternation could be put into words, we had walked away.

Two days later we were informed that the permission for an affidavit in lieu of a baptismal certificate had been granted. Sitting in Groppi's Garden, we toasted my idea. 'Was it just a bluff?' asked Oliver.

'Yes, and no,' was my reply.

'Well, anyway, you took the trick,' he conceded generously.

In the end, it was I who caused a postponement. I developed an acute throat infection and was sent to bed and kept in isolation. I tossed and turned under my mosquito net, frustration as well as fever causing my restlessness. I fretted to think of the passing hours that should have been spent with Oliver.

Gladys became a go-between, carrying notes, messages,

flowers. At the sight of her solid, reassuring figure in the doorway, I forgot the pain and the swollen glands that made a caricature of my face. 'Stay there for a few minutes,' I begged. 'Tell me, what does the doctor really say about me?'

Happily for me, the infection subsided in a matter of days. I was up on the roof my first day of convalescence, waiting for Gladys to bring Oliver up for our first sight of each other since the disaster struck, when Matron appeared.

'The doctor and I think you should go away for a few days,' she told me. 'Ten days by the sea at Port Said should set you up.'

'Thank you, Matron,' I responded, with rebellion in my heart. To leave Cairo meant to leave Oliver, and to leave Oliver would be like exile to the mountains of the moon. Matron left, and depression settled on me like a cold dark cloud.

'You look a bit washed out,' said Oliver. There he stood beside me, and the cloud vanished as he threw a bunch of flowers into my lap and stooped to kiss me. He pulled an empty deck chair close to mine. But when I told him about Port Said, my eyes filled with tears.

He made no comment. Taha appeared with two glasses on a tray. 'Miss Thackray, she say lemon drink good.' His white teeth gleamed in his brown face. 'Maître Moriarty looks fine,' he said, with a dignified bow.

We sipped our lemonade in silence, then Oliver turned to me. 'How about my coming with you?' he asked. 'A long weekend by the sea would be the very thing. Remember, what's sauce for the goose is sauce for the gander.'

So it was settled. Gladys came to see us off at the station. 'A pre-honeymoon,' she said with a smile. 'But don't go too far,' she added. And as the train pulled away from the platform she stood waving until we lost sight of her round the bend.

The week glitters in my memory like the diamonds and sapphires in my ring. I had a room booked for me in the YWCA hostel. It was a room for two, with bunk beds, but as the hostel was half-empty I had it to myself. Beside the door hung a set of rules. As I read them, I began to feel as if I were back in training school; in by ten o'clock; meals out only by permission of the warden.

I read no further. I put my suitcase on the lower bunk and went to find the warden. Night life in Port Said was not likely to start much before ten o'clock, and Oliver and I had planned to have all our meals together. I ran her to earth in the dining room, where she was supervising a native servant who was setting the small single tables for the evening meal.

She turned as I walked in and came towards me. 'Is everything all right?' she asked anxiously.

'Oh, yes,' I said quickly. 'Everything's fine. I'm going to like being here. Only—'

She interrupted me. 'Come and sit over here.'

She led me to a deep window seat. Her appearance left one guessing. She might have been a woman of thirty, or forty, or fifty. Her smooth face was unlined, but somewhere along the road she had lost her youth, or the illusion of youth. Her hair was cut short – 'bobbed' – and there were a few grey hairs amongst the pretty natural waves. She was an attractive woman who seemed to have lost heart where looks were concerned. 'How can I help you?' she asked.

Her blue eyes looked into my grey eyes, and we both liked what we saw. Explaining was easy. 'Don't worry,' she told me, 'for this weekend you will sleep here and breakfast here, and we shall not see you until ten o'clock at night. I'm afraid that rule will have to stand – no getting around that. So, have a happy time together and, remember, I am always here to listen and to help.' There was not a trace of narrow evangelism in her warm smile. One day, I promised myself, she'll tell me the story behind the sadness at the back of those eyes.

Those days together seemed to have the quality of eternity for Oliver and me. We lay amongst the sand dunes and made love – to the limits of our self-imposed standards. We swam in the warm caressing waters of the Mediterranean, and we danced to within minutes of that inexorable ten o'clock. It was the only boulder in our rose-strewn path. Every evening, when Oliver walked me back to the hostel and I watched him walk away, I felt the pangs of an unreasoning jealousy. Would he return to his hotel and dance the night through with someone else? Someone more sophisticated, alluring, charming? Or would he walk along by the edge of the moonlit waves and think of me?

I never asked him, because with the morning light all these painful fantasies had vanished. When Oliver left Port Said, I had absorbed so much happiness that I was able to be philosophical about the remainder of my stay in the now undiluted atmosphere of the YWCA. Also, I found a girlfriend with whom I could enjoy the tourist aspect of Port Said. Ann Keeting was waiting for a ship to take her home after three years of teaching in Cairo.

There was only one last problem. The doctor had ordered me to drink one bottle of Guinness every day. 'Nothing like it, Sister. Picks you up in no time.' Well, that pronouncement was all very well for me, but it gave my friend the warden a headache.

'We are strictly a teetotal establishment,' she told me. 'Yes, I do think we should obey the orders of a doctor, but you cannot bring a bottle of strong drink to the table – it's unthinkable.' She paused, her concerned face wrinkled into a frown of concentration. Then the frown vanished. 'But,' she said, 'if you drink the stout mid-morning and hide the bottle under your bed, that could be the solution.'

And it was. Every morning I drank my stout and lay on my bed until the mild intoxication passed off. As a consequence, the day before I left I presented the warden with another problem: what to do about the 'empties' under my bed? Once again, she came up with a solution. 'Tonight,' she said, 'there will be a full moon. When everyone is in bed and lights are out, we'll take these bottles and bury them in the sand.'

So we did just that. We left the hostel by a back door, each carrying a basket, and walked swiftly along the strip of beach, now the scene of moonlight bathing for the guests from the waterfront hotels. Land crabs scuttled away as our shadows fell across the sand dunes, where we finally came to a halt.

I put my basket down and looked out at the lazy, phosphorescent sea, silvered by the moon. Our mission seemed an anticlimax to this scene of romantic beauty, and I said as much to my companion. She smiled. 'There is another side to everything in life,' she said. 'This does seem absurd, but we really are covering up for a principle.' She picked up a piece of driftwood and started to dig a hole in the fine, silvery sand.

This woman had followed rules all her life, but interpreted them to suit a wider Christian concept, one that would satisfy her own love for the entire human race. I am convinced that had I come to her and said, 'I am not married, and I am going to have a baby; can you help?' she would have come up with a solution.

179

We finished our task and turned back. Just before we reached the hostel, she suddenly gripped my hand. 'God bless you,' she said. 'May you be happy. I lost my man, and my happiness, in the war.'

29

The old saw about the slip 'twixt the cup and the lip has been true since the beginning of time. Oliver and I, getting to know each other those last hectic days before the final step, argued, adjusted, even quarrelled, but we never seemed to lose sight of the essential trust that is part of love. Until right out the blue skies of happiness dropped a bomb named Miss Le Louby. I never knew her first name, nor, indeed, her nationality.

It was one morning when I was off duty. Oliver was taking me to chose my wedding dress. I warned him that I was not going to float up the aisle in white, wearing an absurd veil on my head; 'I'm a working woman, not some fairy-tale princess.'

'It isn't what you show, but what you hide, that matters to me,' he retorted. 'Dress in purple trimmed with sequins if you like, my love.'

After he had tackled the crazy traffic of the Kasr el Nil bridge, I asked, 'How about blue? A blue and white dress like the sky overhead. What do you think?'

'What I have always thought,' and for a second he took one hand from the wheel to touch one of mine. 'I don't care what you put on top of that beautiful body.'

'And a big floppy hat,' I added, recovering from his bit of realism.

'Or one of those flowery trifles we saw at the races on Saturday. Remember?'

I laughed. 'No, I haven't got that sort of a face.'

We turned off the wide boulevard known as the Sharia Suliman Pasha and stopped in front of a small boutique. Above the door was written 'Leroux', in a sort of arrogant simplicity. 'A satisfied client of mine,' explained Oliver. 'I winched her out of a legal tangle and she is dying to meet you.'

Madame Leroux did, indeed, welcome us. Little excited exclamations accompanied us around the shop's interior. 'Bien, bien!' she said, shaking a finger at Oliver. 'Bad boy! He has at last brought you to see an old friend. *Vraiment!* I will make you a bride more beautiful than you deserve.'

This little dumpy woman was a symphony in black: black silk dress, jet-black beads, sparkling black eyes. We spent an hour or more with her, trying on and rejecting until finally she was satisfied. I hardly seemed to count.

'This is it,' she said, standing back, her head on one side. 'We look no more.' Then, as an afterthought, she added, quite simply, 'You like it, yes?'

While her assistant made up the parcel, laying the chosen dress in its long box with rustling tissue paper between each careful fold, Madame Leroux took us into a dark room at the back of the shop to drink an aperitif.

Oliver and I ended that morning by sinking into two wicker chairs in Groppi's Garden, tilting the big table umbrella to give us a little shade against Egypt's merciless noonday sun. 'You made a good impression, darling,' he said with approval, as we mopped our faces and sipped our cool drinks. 'Madame Leroux's sharp little eyes miss nothing, and even an Irish cattle dealer can't make a sounder judgement.'

'Thanks for the compliment,' I said, smiling.

'You needn't be snooty – the greatest of these, is an Irish cattle dealer.' After which cryptic remark he was silent.

A shadow passed across our table, and I looked up to see a small dark person looking at Oliver as if she were about to speak. He stiffened, but showed no other sign of recognition, and she passed on. Her companion was a swarthy young Egyptian wearing a tarbush set at a jaunty angle. They sat down at an adjacent table.

I was perturbed; something that I did not understand had passed between Oliver and this woman. Yet he made no comment as he took a cigarette from his case and lit it. And then – 'A fragment from my past,' he said casually. 'How about a sandwich with our drinks?' and he beckoned the waiter to give the order.

If that was how he wanted it, I could act indifference as well as he. I looked at my watch. 'It'll have to be a quick one,' I said, 'or I'll be late back on duty.' I was conscious that we were being watched by the dark woman in the crimson dress. My sandwich tasted like sawdust, but I ate it as if I enjoyed every bit. Oliver had that brooding look I had begun to recognize, signifying that he was thinking out some problem.

When we had finished our quick meal, he stood up. 'I want you to meet Miss Le Louby.' And, to my consternation, he led me over to the table where the woman in the crimson dress was sitting.

The cat at the mousehole, I thought, with inconsequential bitterness. A minute later, and she was calling him 'Ollie'. I froze. I felt trapped in a web of jealousy and mistrust. What was she saying? 'Sit down. I have to talk to you, Ollie. I need your help. My case comes up in two weeks. You will defend. Yes?'

Oliver looked dubious and, I was glad to see, uncomfortable. 'We can't discuss it here and now. Come to my office tomorrow evening. My fiancée is a Sister at the Anglo-American Hospital, and I have to get her back on duty on time.'

'Fiancée? Congratulations.' Her sharp black eyes were assessing my points as a woman. She laid a small claw-like hand with hennaed nails on the sleeve of the young man beside her. 'Mohammed here thinks he is going to marry me. Who knows? Maybe yes; maybe no. I am not the marrying kind. Perhaps one day I change my mind. *Chi lo sa?*' Her laugh was more derisive than amused. As we walked away, I could feel her eyes, mocking and triumphant at the realization of my embarrassment.

Oliver waited until I was sitting beside him in the car. 'What the devil upset you?' he demanded. He swerved to avoid an Arab on a donkey who was happily zigzagging across the road.

'I don't know,' I replied. But my face flushed crimson, because I did know. This denial was just a cowardly retreat from confrontation.

'If you resent Miss Le Louby, forget it.' He paused. Then, abruptly, he said, 'When I first came out here she was my mistress.' He believed in calling a spade a spade, but I still dodged behind Victorian convention, and I was shocked.

'It's all over,' he continued, swerving again to avoid a woman balancing a basket of fruit on her head. 'Miss Le Louby is a decent sort. You needn't worry. When I tell you it's over, it is just that. Either you trust me, or you don't. And I'm not marrying someone who does not trust me. Which is it to be?'

In a frightened whisper, I replied once again, 'I – I don't know.'

'The bloody hell you don't!' he rasped. 'Well, I do.'

Neither of us spoke again. He left me at the hospital, and drove away without another word or look.

That night I hardly slept. I knew how vital my reaction was to this situation. Without trust, what hope was there of happiness? What hope was there in any case? Had I not already cut the lifelines with my stupid 'I don't know'?

After dawn came, I slept a brief, uneasy sleep. But when I woke in the morning, I saw, sharp and clear, the testing point on which my decision would rest. Oliver had said that this affair with Miss Le Louby was over. But if he defended her in this case of which she had spoken, they would have to meet, to talk. Why should she pick on him? Why should he take the case? There were other lawyers in Cairo, and dying embers can be fanned into flames. If he refused to take her case, that would be the guarantee for our marriage. Trust would be firmly established from that moment.

I went down to breakfast like someone in a dream, hoping no-one would notice or comment on the dark rings under my eyes. But routine is the greatest healer of all; by the end of the day I had adjusted to the empty feeling of my new position in life, be it temporary or permanent. I felt isolated, though, for I could not talk about it, even to Thackray. How could a Victorian leftover like myself discuss the question of my fiancé's former mistress, and the fact that he had introduced her to me? And how could I make the first move? After all, didn't a man have to take the initiative in most things? I was an odd mixture. In some ways I had begun to think in the modern way, and in others I was a true product of my generation.

As the days passed there was no sign of Oliver. I lost hope. I told myself it was all over, my marriage had been a dream that burst. But I didn't believe it; I waited for a letter, a telephone call. And then it came – the summons to the phone.

My hand shook as I held the receiver. Oliver's voice! This was the moment I had longed for, yet dreaded. I remember thinking, as I listened, that he sounded as if nothing had happened, as if there had been no doubt and no agony. 'Darling, that case is off. Finished! Kaput! Do you understand?'

Idiotically, I found myself nodding assent. I was dizzy with relief. Life could go on. 'Yes,' I said, and the calmness of my voice surprised me.

'So I pick you up at seven?' he continued. 'I do? That "yes" is

184

the second word you've spoken. *Malesh* – no matter. We'll make up for it tonight. Wear that pale blue affair – we're going to Shepheards, and I want to show you off.'

One of his good points – he always noticed what I wore.

30

Once again, Aunt Gertie popped into my life. Evidently, with my mother's letter telling her of the news of my engagement, she had begun organizing my arrangements. She remembered that the wife of one of the Residency officials was a Catholic and, more important, an 'old girl' of Aunt Gertie's Holy Child convent school. This time I let myself be propelled by her plans. I was to be married from their house.

They were a childless couple; delightful people, who spent their spare time doing those quiet kindnesses that people with families have no time for. The husband was a conventional government official type, who wore the 'old school tie' with quiet assurance – a likeable man by any standard. Gwendoline, his wife, was really lovely, in the madonna tradition. In the short while since I first met them, the acquaintance had been hurried into a friendship by the connection to Aunt Gertie.

The wedding was to be in two parts: the consular marriage one day, and the religious ceremony in the cathedral on the following day. When Gwendoline fetched me from the hospital, the day before the wedding, I had the feeling of being married from my own home. After I had gone to bed, that first night in their house, there was a gentle tap at my door. I was sitting up in bed rereading my last letter from home. 'Come in,' I invited, putting the letter down.

Gwendoline came in and sat down beside me, but her face looked troubled, and there was obviously something on her mind. Had something gone wrong with the arrangements? I wondered. 'I thought—' she started, then stopped. 'I was wondering,' she went on, 'if you feel as frightened as I did, the day before my wedding? I expect I am quite wrong in this, only—' A slow flush of embarrassment had spread over her lovely face. So *that* was the reason for her visit, to find out if I was fully aware of the facts of life.

'Don't worry,' I told her, 'I am not a young girl. I am a nurse who took her midwifery exam. I know what you are trying to tell me, and I do appreciate your concern.'

She gave a sigh of relief as she got up, took my hand, and kissed me. 'We have been so happy,' she said, 'and I do hope you will be the same.'

Dear Gwendoline. We were not really married, by her reckoning, until the Church had given its blessing. After the civil ceremony, she took me to spend the rest of the day in the Sporting Club. She was taking no chances.

There were no trimmings to the service in the cathedral. We had firmly refused the red carpet and the 'Wedding March'. Just a handful of close friends came to see us married, and to wish us luck.

'You look lovely,' said Gladys. 'But then I knew you would. I shall miss you.' We were standing on the steps of the cathedral, waiting for Oliver to bring the car round. 'You will be our first guest,' I told her. 'Always welcome.'

As the car came to a stop and I got in beside Oliver, the little group of friends cheered and waved, and someone threw rice, which pattered like hail on my floppy hat. Instantly, skinny little brown figures came rushing up, even climbing on to the dashboard, to scrape up a few grains 'Backsheesh, Backsheesh,' they cried as Oliver pressed the starter. As we drove away, he threw a handful of silver while the little urchins dropped off. 'Poor little devils,' he said. 'Our Protectorate doesn't do much to protect them from hunger and poverty.'

We left the city behind. We were rushing in our open car along the road to the Mena House Hotel beside the Sphinx. The tall jacaranda trees that lined the road seemed to be hurrying to meet us.

There was one terrifying moment when I turned my head to look at the man by my side, his confident hands on the wheel, and I saw him as a stranger. But that terrifying moment passed. This was my husband, and at the end of this long straight road, we were going to find happiness and fulfilment. I looked at the gold ring on my finger.

'It's up to you now,' whispered Destiny, disappearing in a cloud of dust.

Afterword

When I left Egypt in 1926 I took with me a year-old baby son. We stayed with my parents in Gravesend, or with our old family friends, the Masons, in Ditchling, the lovely village outside Brighton. Oliver stayed behind to clear up our affairs in Cairo. And then moved to Ireland, to pick up his practice on the Munster Circuit.

I had always scribbled and written poems and fairy tales. Now, with loving people taking on the baby-sitting of Bernard, I set to work to write my first novel, *The Shadow of the Pyramid*, which was published by Hurst and Blackett in 1928. I can see myself in the evenings, sitting in a gas-lit corridor outside the room where my son lay sleeping. Repainting the Egyptian scene and background, creating people and situations. It was a peaceful way of life.

Followed by thirty years in Southern Ireland. Thirty years of challenges. Inspiration now switched from pen and paper to daily living: to bringing up two sons; to keeping a home together. Making bookcases from orange boxes and visiting Dublin's junk shops. Paying bills when there was no money. To making warm and loving friends when I had little to give in return.

For Oliver was an alcoholic. A brilliant brain; a voice, as someone put it, 'To charm the birds off the trees'. But with a drink problem for which I had to cover up. And a health problem dating from the faulty surgery in the Anglo-American Hospital.

I often wonder myself how I coped. To begin with, I found an utterly loyal and faithful maid called Mary, and with her co-operation I returned to part-time nursing: odd jobs for the local doctors and night duty; mostly comforting the last hours of the dying. But there was also glove-making for Switzers, one of the big stores; clerical work in the offices of the Irish Sweepstake; and broadcasting my own script from Radio Eireann during the war. Finally I ran an unofficial nursing home for the elderly, starting, in partnership with a nurse friend, an agency to provide home care for the old who lived in a fantasy world and drove their caring relatives up the wall. In between all this, I managed a couple of mastectomies for myself, as well as severe sinus trouble!

Out of that part-time nursing I made a solicitor friend, whose daughter – according to him – I nursed back to life and fulfilment. When Oliver died, Terence Doyle got me made an annuitant of RUKBA, blackmailing his clients to give me their votes which were, at that time, needed for an applicant to be accepted.

Now, in my hundredth year, I look back and can truthfully say *Deo Gratias*. For I have always had love; and the one thing I had to give was love. And that love of yesterday pays dividends in the love that now envelops me. Love of sons, of daughters-in-law, of grandchildren.

So I do believe in Destiny? I do. When I lived in Ireland (which I did for thirty years), we had an old friend we called 'Aunt Jane Green'. We all poured our troubles into her sympathetic ears. Her unvarying response was, 'It was meant, dear.'

Yes, Aunt Jane Green. You were right. 'It was meant.'

Te Deum laudamus.

Edwin Lutyens
by Mary Lutyens

Lutyen's pre-eminence among English architects was unquestioned during his lifetime and today his genius is universally acknowledged. Honours and commissions were showered upon him in what was seemingly a life of dazzling success. The variety and extent of his work are astonishing: country houses; collaboration with Gertrude Jekyll on designing gardens for houses and houses for gardens; Castle Drogo in Devonshire; New Delhi; the Cenotaph and the designs for the Roman Catholic Cathedral in Liverpool.

Yet at the core of this fun-loving, childlike and often frivolous public figure were intense private disappointments, anxieties and frustrations. Conflicting forces flawed his marriage to a woman he passionately loved; his one relationship outside it was poignantly unsatisfactory; his greatest work, at New Delhi, was marred by his failure to inspire others with his brilliantly conceived ideals.

The subject of his daughter's memoir is the man himself, revealed through her own memories and her parents' letters to each other. Many readers will feel, as the drama evolves, that Lutyen's nobility of character transcends even his genius and his charm.

'Fascinating in itself and valuable for what it reveals of the oddity and agony of a creative individual . . . Mary Lutyens has given us a most vivid portrait of her father'
Listener

'Splendid occasions with splendid people come freshly from her recollections'
Sir John Summerson, *The Times Literary Supplement*

0 552 99417 0

BLACK SWAN

A SELECTION OF BIOGRAPHIES AND AUTOBIOGRAPHIES AVAILABLE FROM CORGI AND BLACK SWAN

THE PRICES SHOWN BELOW WERE CORRECT AT THE TIME OF GOING TO PRESS. HOWEVER TRANSWORLD PUBLISHERS RESERVE THE RIGHT TO SHOW NEW RETAIL PRICES ON COVERS WHICH MAY DIFFER FROM THOSE PREVIOUSLY ADVERTISED IN THE TEXT OR ELSEWHERE.

□	99315 8	NO TIME FOR ROMANCE	Lucilla Andrews	£3.95
□	99065 5	THE PAST IS MYSELF	Christabel Bielenberg	£3.95
□	13588 7	DAUGHTER OF SHANGHAI	Tsai Chin	£3.99
□	13126 1	CATHERINE COOKSON COUNTRY	Catherine Cookson	£5.95
□	13582 8	THE GOD SQUAD	Paddy Doyle	£3.99
□	13070 2	BORN LUCKY: AN AUTOBIOGRAPHY	John Francome	£2.95
□	12833 3	THE HOUSE BY THE DVINA	Eugenie Fraser	£4.99
□	99347 6	A TIME TO DANCE, NO TIME TO WEEP	Rumer Godden	£4.99
□	13586 0	SUSAN'S STORY	Susan Hampshire	£2.99
□	12863 5	THE LONG JOURNEY HOME	Flora Leipman	£3.95
□	13550 X	DIANA'S STORY	Deric Longden	£3.50
□	13374 4	HOUSE OF TOMORROW	Claire Lorrimer	£3.95
□	99336 0	TO BE YOUNG	Mary Lutyens	£3.50
□	99417 0	EDWIN LUTYENS	Mary Lutyens	£5.99
□	13567 4	COMRADE PRINCESS	Princess Mescherskaya	£4.99
□	99333 6	NO GOING BACK TO MOLDOVA	Anna Robertson	£3.99
□	13732 4	A MOTHER'S WAR	Fey Von Hassell	£4.99
□	12072 3	KITCHEN IN THE HILLS	Elizabeth West	£2.50
□	11707 2	GARDEN IN THE HILLS	Elizabeth West	£2.50
□	10907 X	HOVEL IN THE HILLS	Elizabeth West	£2.99
□	13347 7	INSUFFERABLE LITTLE CHILDREN	Elizabeth West	£2.99

All Corgi/Bantam Books are available at your bookshop or newsagent, or can be ordered from the following address:

Corgi/Bantam Books,
Cash Sales Department
P.O. Box 11, Falmouth, Cornwall TR10 9EN

Please send a cheque or postal order (no currency) and allow 80p for postage and packing for the first book plus 20p for each additional book ordered up to a maximum charge of £2.00 in UK.

B.F.P.O. customers please allow 80p for the first book and 20p for each additional book.

Overseas customers, including Eire, please allow £1.50 for postage and packing for the first book, £1.00 for the second book, and 30p for each subsequent title ordered.

NAME (Block Letters) ....

ADDRESS ....

....